Simon Blackburn is Distinguished Research Professor at the University of North Carolina, and Professor of Philosophy at the New College of the Humanities. He was, for many years, Professor of Philosophy at the University of Cambridge, and is one of the most distinguished philosophers writing today. He is the author of the bestselling books *The Oxford Dictionary of Philosophy*, *Think*, *Being Good*, *Lust*, *Truth: A Guide for the Perplexed* and *How to Read Hume*. He lives in Cambridge.

WHAT DO WE REALLY KNOW?

THE BIG QUESTIONS OF PHILOSOPHY

SIMON BLACKBURN

Quercus

This paperback edition published in 2012 by
Quercus
55 Baker Street
Seventh Floor, South Block
London
W1U 8EW

Hardback edition originally published by Quercus in 2009 as
THE BIG QUESTIONS: Philosophy

A CIP catalogue record for this book is available
from the British Library

ISBN 978 1 78087 587 3

10 9 8 7 6 5 4 3

Designed and typeset by Ellipsis Digital Ltd

Printed and bound in Great Britain by Clays Ltd. St Ives plc

Contents

Preface

The twenty questions I have chosen here are among those that often occur to thoughtful men, women and children. They seem to arise naturally, with our powers of reflection. We want to know the answers. Yet philosophy is unusual among academic disciplines in appearing to cherish the questions rather than provide the answers. The tradition contains few agreed and definitive solutions. This may be a matter of regret or embarrassment to those of us who work as academic philosophers, but I do not think it should be. This is partly because some questions which appear simple and straightforward at first glance fragment into many other little questions on reflection. We ask, 'Why be moral?' or 'What is the meaning of life?' as if one answer might be around the corner. But perhaps there are many different questions. Why be moral in this particular way on this particular occasion, faced with this, that or the other temptation? Which of the things that can interest and engage people deserve to do so? There will be many answers in different contexts, rather than one big answer, and it is progress to realize this.

Other questions may have different concealed traps in them. 'Why is there something rather than nothing?' is a good example. Although it is sometimes thought to be the fundamental question of philosophy, the deepest question anyone can ask, it may be that its depth, and the obsessive interest it can engender, are the artefact of a logical trick ensuring that it is unanswerable. Or perhaps not: these are matters on which we have to tread carefully, and not all thinkers will tread the same path. I do not think we should lament that or be embarrassed about that. We would not all tread the same path if we tried to write essays about almost any human affairs: just imagine the different lights in which a political decision or a family holiday (or family quarrel) may appear to different participants and observers. Shakespeare wrote wonderful plays about love, war, fear, ambition and many other things, but nobody believes that he gave definitive 'answers' or that there is nothing left to add.

So I have tried to acquaint the reader with the questions, with some of the things that get said, and with some of the pitfalls and perplexities surrounding them.

The twenty questions I have chosen are here arranged in no particular order, except for the last one, which comes last for all of us. The discussions are intended to be self-contained, and therefore readers are welcome to dip in wherever they wish. Since there are occasional cross-references, they may find themselves drawn backwards or forwards as the case may be, and I hope that they are.

The 21st century continues a trend also visible in the last century. This is a certain kind of scientific triumphalism. The euphoria that came with cracking the human genome, and the dazzling prospects of unlimited biological and medical progress that this encouraged, have contributed to an atmosphere in which humane studies like philosophy are put on the defensive.

Insofar as we philosophers do things like interpreting human nature, then is philosophy itself due for retirement, overtaken and superseded by the juggernaut of advancing science? In a number of chapters I reflect on the actual achievements and promises of the new sciences of human nature, not always with quite the confidence that others seem to feel. I hope that the reasons in play at least raise some doubts, and enable others to approach the difficult problems of how we do think and feel, and then how we ought to think and feel, with proper respect.

I owe thanks to my agent, Catherine Clarke, and to my editor at Quercus, Wayne Davies, for unfailing encouragement. I owe thanks, as ever, to my wife whose editorial and literary help have been invaluable. The University of Cambridge granted me a sabbatical term in 2008 which gave me the leisure to write many of the following chapters, while the University of North Carolina at Chapel Hill provided a research chair from which to work, and I am most grateful to both institutions.

Am I A Ghost in a Machine?
The search for consciousness

Everyone knows that we are creatures of flesh and blood. Included in the flesh is a nice big brain, an unimaginably complex assemblage of some hundred billion neurons or brain cells, each with around a thousand connections with others: many trillions of connections in all.

The human brain controls memory, vision, learning, thought and voluntary behaviour. It also monitors and plays a part in controlling the involuntary behaviour and the autonomic activities of our organic support systems. Different sense organs respond to physical stimuli, and thence transmit signals to dedicated parts of the brain, which then work together to enable us to see, feel, taste, smell, remember and compare and classify things. Most of the time it all works magically well, and we only get a sense of its wonderfully fragile nature when things go wrong. A small amount of neuronal damage, and we have people who think that the person in the mirror is not themselves but someone different, or who cannot remember who or where they are, or who think their wife is a hat. A small shadow on a scan, and Alzheimer's terrifyingly awaits a great many of us.

The inner world

This is the physical basis of our lives as conscious, thinking, active animals. But there is a temptation to think: that's fine as a basis, but *then what*? What is it the basis *of*? We could chase, say, an optical stimulation from the time a light ray hits our eyes, on to a pattern of activation of cells in the retina, on to excitations in the optic nerve, back into increased activity in the visual cortex, and thence, perhaps, into a diffusion of excitements across different parts of the entire system. But where in all this is the fact of me, say, seeing a car passing? How does the conscious experience arise or emerge from the fantastic physical system? And in our imaginings there is then a kind of secondary, superadded world. This is the world of our 'inner' experience, our imaginings, feelings, thoughts and sense experiences: our own private take on things.

We go on to think that my inner world is accessible to me and yours is accessible to you. But yours is not accessible to me, or not in the same way that it is to you or that mine is to me. We have privileged access to our own mental states. You, as scientist, might be able to chart the excitation patterns in my brain. But it is I, the subject, who sees the car passing. And you do not see my sight of that, however closely you pry into my brain, or however accurately you plot the way the cells are doing their dance. Our mental states are themselves invisible to the best sciences of the brain. Suppose I think about the boulevards of Paris, pleasurably laying them out in my mind's eye as I imagine strolling down them. The neurophysiologist, however far he probes, will not be able to hold up a fragment of brain and say, 'Aha! Here we have a thought about the boulevards of Paris!' For, alas, the brain is grey but in my thoughts the boulevards are brightly coloured. The bit of brain is small, but the boulevards are long and wide. The brain is soft tissue, while in my daydream the boulevards are hard pavement, and with traffic on them.

Such thoughts are natural enough, but rapidly lead to insoluble puzzles. At the beginning of the scientific revolution of the 17th century they led René Descartes to postulate a part of the brain (he fixed on something called the pineal gland) as a kind of gateway to the soul. The you, or self, resided behind this portal, and the brain brought messages to you, while you could issue dictates to it, thereby initiating a train of events that might lead to your walking or talking or even becoming irritated at the problem of consciousness. This is the model that Gilbert Ryle, in the 20th century, called that of the 'ghost in the machine'. The brain–body system is a giant machine; its function is to bring information to the ghost, and to transmit back instructions from him. Descartes actually denied that he wanted a model of the self residing in the body like a pilot in a ship, but basically that is the image he has left us.

God's good pleasure

Thinking of consciousness like this is highly unsatisfactory. It clearly clips the wings of science rather dramatically. On this model it turns out that however much neuroscience learns, there will always be the closed door, the portal to the world of consciousness, and behind that closed door a world with utterly mysterious connections with the physical world. The world of the ghost is shut off from scientific inquiry. But so is the system whereby the ghost is connected with the body, a whole new set of laws and forces about which we are doomed to know nothing. Neither science nor philosophy likes to be told of such no-go areas in our attempts to understand the world.

Although the last decade of the last century has been called the decade of consciousness studies, with a wide variety of contributions from a wide variety of disciplines, the basic philosophical options were laid down not long after Descartes first wrote. They emerge in a dialogue between John Locke, who followed Descartes's model, and Gottfried Wilhelm Leibniz. When Locke confronted the question of why a particular sensation, such as feeling a pin prick, should arise from a particular excitation pattern in the physical world, he could only say that it was 'God's good pleasure' to make the association, this being a colourful way of saying that we cannot know anything about it. Leibniz, more optimistic perhaps about the powers of human understanding (see *Why Is There Something and Not Nothing?*), replied:

> It must not be thought that ideas such as those of colour and pain are arbitrary and that between them and their causes there is no relation or natural connection: it is not God's way to act in such an unruly and unreasoned fashion. I would say, rather, that there is a resemblance of a kind – not a perfect one which holds all the way through, but a resemblance in which one thing expresses another through some orderly relationship between them. Thus an ellipse, and even a parabola or hyperbola, has some resemblance to the circle of which it is a projection on a plane ... it is true that pain does not

resemble the movement of a pin; but it might thoroughly resemble the motions which the pin causes in our body, and might represent them in the soul; and I have not the least doubt that it does.

For Locke, it is as if God had to do three things: make a physical world, make the world of conscious experience, and then make some bridging laws linking one to the other. Leibniz says he has only to do one thing: make a physical world, and the rest follows on in the way that geometrical consequences follow their premises. Once God (nature) has generated a right-angled triangle, he or it does not have to do anything else to ensure that the square on the hypotenuse is the sum of the squares on the other two sides. Leibniz wants it to be like this, pinpointing exactly what we need: the 'world' of conscious experience has to be put into an intelligible relationship with that of physics and neuroscience.

Mary, spectra, zombies

So it is not much good only being told that our thoughts 'emerge' from particular combinations of brain excitations. They may 'supervene' on them, to use a popular philosophical term, meaning that there is no change in thought without an underlying change in the state of the brain. But it is little help to say such things if at the end of the day we can understand nothing about how this emergence takes place, or what the conscious world is that indeed emerges. This is the same counsel of despair as Locke's stopping with 'God's good pleasure'. Leibniz insists on

a more transparent understanding than that. He wants to close
what more recent philosophers have called the 'explanatory gap'.

There are a number of arguments (sometimes referred to
pejoratively as 'intuition pumps') that are designed to make us
keep the explanatory gap open. One is the fantasy of the zombie:
the thought experiment of a creature that is physically just like
us, but in whom the portal to the world of conscious experience
is shut. This creature behaves like you and me, but all without
consciousness. It has no inner life, only the outward appearances
of one. On Locke's view, God can make zombies. A second
thought experiment is that of the 'inverted spectrum'. Here you
are to imagine a person whose physical structures are just like
yours, but who sees colours in a systematically inverted way.
Colours you see towards the blue end of the spectrum, he or she
sees towards the red end, and vice versa. Physically, again, he is
just like you, but things look different to him and his conscious
life is very different. A third thought experiment introduces
something known as 'Frank Jackson's knowledge argument', after
it was unveiled in a seminal paper by the Australian philosopher
Frank Jackson. In his story Mary is an incredibly knowledgeable
physical scientist who knows everything there is to know about
physics, chemistry, the workings of the human brain and human
behavioural responses to things. But she has been kept all her life
in a monochrome room. One day she is released, and for the first
time in her life sees a banana. 'Aha!' she says to herself, 'So that's
what it's like to see the colour yellow! I have often wondered.' The
intuition here is that Mary indeed learns something new. There
is an 'Aha!' moment signalling a new arrival in her conscious
inner theatre, and she could not have told what it would be like,

however much she knew about rods and cones in the eye, or the best theories of how the eye–brain system reacts to light of different energies at different wavelengths. This predictive gap is the same as the explanatory gap.

Many philosophers want to fight back, with Leibniz, against the direction in which these intuition pumps push us. Perhaps the most obvious reason for doing so is that it leaves us in despair about the minds of others. If zombies are possible, then how do I know that you are not one? If everything I can ever detect in your doings and sayings leaves it open whether you are conscious, why even suppose that you are? Perhaps it was God's good pleasure to make me the only conscious being amongst billions of zombies. Or perhaps his well-known goodness brings it about that only people leading relatively nice lives are conscious, and the poor and neglected of the world are fortunately unconscious and aware of nothing.

If inverted spectra are possible then, again, you may be the proud possessor of one. Perhaps we could bite this bullet and reflect sadly that perhaps we do know less about others than we like to think. But it is worse than that. In one of his most brilliant arguments, Ludwig Wittgenstein pressed the question into our own case. How do I know that I see colours the way I did yesterday? How do I know that I was conscious during my life until this moment? It is no good answering that my memories assure me of these things. Perhaps my present neurology is indeed modified by the whole train of physical events that have happened to my brain and body until now. And perhaps it is now delivering messages up through the portal of consciousness, including messages assuring me, in my thoughts, that I do see colours as I saw them yesterday, or that I was conscious during the decades of my life before now. But why take memory to be reliable on that? Perhaps the portals of consciousness do not open all that often, but just now I am under the illusion that my own were always open even during times when they were not! After all, there is no theory, on this account, of how conscious-ness manages to leave traces of itself. We know that memory is generally entirely dependent on well-functioning neurophysi-ology, and so far as we can tell it takes physical energies to have cellular effects. So perhaps consciousness cannot leave traces and never does, and we live under the perpetual illusion that we have been conscious up until the present, just as we now are.

Fighting back

Surely this will not do. Back, then, to Leibniz. How is his intelli-gible relationship to be found? Let us consider the three intuition pumps one by one. Zombies? I find it amusing that when I explain the zombie thought experiment to a class, most students find it convincing. If I then ask them how zombies move, most of them do a stiff parody of Frankenstein's monster, lumbering and lurching around in a kind of mechanical, automated way. If asked how zombies talk, they come up with something sounding like a computerized telephone answering system, monotonic, expressionless and mechanical. But that's wrong! Zombies are supposed to move and talk like the rest of us! But now think of our own activities. We show quick attention, flexible smiles, flashes of understanding, agile appreciation of situations and jokes, indefinitely controlled movements, puzzled frowns and a great variety of emotions, moods, attitudes and feelings. Our faces alone picture our thought processes with wonderful precision. If we think about this, something like Leibniz's geometrical analogy begins to come into view: our consciousness is *expressed* in our faces and movements, and perhaps the relation is intelligible in just the way that the circle and the ellipse are in his example. We know what our friend's conscious life *must be* like if we see him dejected and fighting back tears after some blow or her sudden dawning appreciation of a joke. And then the zombie possibility begins to fade: a creature whose quick smile, dart of recognition, frowns and postures are indistinguishable from ours is expressing what we express. He is animated, just as we are. My students' zombies differed exactly in not being animated at all.

The inverted spectrum raises a host of fascinating questions that can only be indicated here. First of all, it is telling that it is always colour inversion that presents itself as possible. It is harder to be captivated by the idea that there might be a creature indistinguishable from me who has tone inversion (so what I hear as a low growl he hears as a high squeak, and vice versa). Or one who sees as black what I see as white, for that matter. This last might quickly seem incoherent. Is he supposed to see things better as the light gets darker? Is night to be like broad daylight, although he stumbles into things just like I do, while daylight to him is like night, although he is much better at avoiding obstacles? Can we really make sense of that? With chromatic vision, it is not so obvious, but similar arguments may well apply. Colours have connections with other aspects of things: red is a warm and exciting colour, yellow is bright, blue dark and green cool, for example. Colours have their own very intricate connections with each other, and it is not at all obvious that a systematic displacement around the colour wheel, but one which leaves all these interrelations intact, is possible. If we put all this together, we might begin to hope that we can indeed 'see' how, once the physics is fixed, so is the way colours look.

If that is so, then Mary's 'Aha!' moment need not be so dramatic. Suppose Mary is presented with a purple banana. She might know she is being tricked. The neurophysiology of our light sensitivity will have told her that there are just four colours that look unique: red, green, yellow and blue. Others look like mixtures, such as purple (red/blue) or orange (red/yellow). Since she is allowed to know beforehand that yellow, whatever it looks like, is a unique bright colour, and that bananas are said to be yellow, she may know, just by looking, that a purple impostor is not an ordinary banana. Perhaps by extending this sort of argument we can diminish the explanatory gap down to the point where Leibniz's ambition becomes realizable.

We have further worries about consciousness. People who have been totally paralysed may remember a fairly rich mental life with no possibility of expressing it, and this too makes it seem as though the mind and the body are very different things. And we see how animals look and behave, yet we somehow feel that their mental lives are opaque to us. At the limits we may wonder whether some creatures are conscious at all. It looks as though the fish on the end of a hook is in pain, but is it? In the way that we would be? It is important to note that this is a different problem. We might get a sense of why someone behaving in every way like a normal person must have the conscious life of a normal person (thereby siding with Leibniz) without quite knowing what to say either about people who in some ways do not behave normally, or about animals who behave differently in any case.

A popular contemporary suggestion is that consciousness comes with a 'higher-order' set of skills of monitoring states of our brains or bodies. It is our awareness of our own damage or our own distress that makes up conscious pain, so while the fish is 'in distress' this may be more like the sense in which a plant without water can be in distress. Descartes managed to convince himself that apart from human beings no other animals were conscious, and others have argued that without language, higher-order thought, and hence consciousness, is impossible. But most of us feel a twinge of unease at these rather speciesist arguments. When it comes to the loyal dog or the miserable-looking ape in the zoo it is hard to think like that. And there is no evolutionary reason to think that consciousness has only the function of monitoring our own states as opposed to also having the function of monitoring the world around us.

I believe that we best approach the nature of consciousness by getting over the idea that the way it is expressed in bodily behaviour is somehow unintelligible. We have to recapture the idea that a smile is an utterly natural mode of expression of pleasure or happiness, so the mental state is not something lying behind the fully functioning individual, but something that is visible in their face or in their doings. It is not accidental, for instance, that someone who feels happy walks with a light step, someone who feels dejected with a heavy step and downcast face. We also have to insist that we do know a lot about the conscious lives of others. Someone who watches the same football match from the adjacent seat sees things in very much the way that I do, unless his attention or experience makes different things salient to him – and that also can be detected.

This approaches something of what Aristotle meant when he said that the mind is the form of the body, and it is telling that the Greeks had no word directly translatable as 'consciousness'. Perhaps they were ahead of us in recognizing that consciousness is not a matter of happenings in a mysterious, parallel world to the one we inhabit. It is simply our animation in that world. So once God, or nature, had made the animated creature, the work was done. There was no second world to add on and no third task of adjusting the two worlds to each other.

What is Human Nature?
The problem of interpretation

Human nature obsesses us, and has always done so. We know about our animal constitutions, in immense scientific and medical detail. But our psychologies are more elusive. We relentlessly interpret and reinterpret ourselves. We are complex, and can surprise each other and ourselves.

We ask whether it is in human nature to be rational or emotional, selfish or altruistic, short-sighted or prudent, aggressive, pacific, promiscuous, monogamous, murderous or moral, and even after years of experience, some say one and some say the other.

Libraries or laboratories?

If years studying history in the library or with anthropologists in the field do not throw up stable answers to these old questions, can experimental methods and science do any better? Sciences, or supposed sciences, are certainly eager to help. Evolutionary psychologists speculate about our hominid ancestors in their Pleistocene environments, while primatologists try to pick up clues about what we are like by looking at chimpanzees and bonobos. Experimental economists have people playing games for pennies, while neurophysiologists interrogate brain scans and social psychologists scatter questionnaires across the world wide web.

Our theories about ourselves matter. If I believe that everyone is ultimately selfish, I will conduct my life differently, and may myself become selfish, untrusting and untrustworthy, and other people may follow suit. If I believe that our genes are our fate and that culture does not matter, I will not willingly pay taxes for schools or care what my children watch on television. A mistaken view of human nature may be the beginning of a downward spiral. So not only are these questions interesting in themselves, but they have a direct practical importance.

Culture and nature

In approaching the area we might first worry whether human nature is even a respectable concept, or merely a remnant of the Aristotelian idea that everything has a fixed natural state. Darwin scotched that, arguing both that species change over time, and that the starting point of the mechanism of change is variation within the species. The function of sexual reproduction and its accompanying genetic recombinations is probably just to help this variation along. Furthermore, the journey from genome to the resulting animal shows no one natural relationship. Often it only shows a variety of outcomes as genes express themselves differently in different environments, and the resulting differences, although not due to genes, can themselves be heritable. All we can hope for is that there are interesting constancies, just as there are other constancies in animal development. Two eyes and two arms are usually fixed, but who is to say which psychological traits are similarly inelastic? Perhaps what is constant is not a simple trait, such as being selfish or aggressive, but an association of environment and the trait, such as being selfish if brought up to be, or aggressive if surrounded by aggressive adults, just as what is constant about language learning is not that children learn French or learn Chinese, but that they learn whichever mother tongue surrounds them.

This should be enough to warn us off the silly view that there is something 'unscientific' about seeing ourselves as partly the result of culture or environment. Culture is not a misty Spirit of the Age, a weird and ghostly causal force above and distinct from the world around us. Appealing to culture is just appealing to the important and pervasive part of the environment that consists in the doings of other people. It is because of culture, in this sense, that we speak the mother tongues we do, admire the things we admire, have the particular hopes and expectations we enjoy. Culture gives Canada one-quarter of the murder rate of the USA, and a few centuries – far too short a period for natural selection to operate – changed bloodthirsty Vikings into today's peaceful Scandinavians.

Various sciences, or a combination of them, may bring advances in our self-understandings. But we must always be careful of confusing science with the ideology of particular scientists. This is particularly true of biology's long affair with the impossibility of altruism. In biological thought, 'altruism' means an action which sacrifices your own fitness for the good of another, and the argument is that any such tendency would be weeded out over evolutionary time. According to this view, the

Darwinian survivor must be the most competitive, aggressive and ruthless beast in the jungle, and might is right or, at any rate, inevitably rules.

Those rampant genes

In his classic book *The Selfish Gene*, the distinguished biologist Richard Dawkins tries to soften this, floating the idea that humans alone on earth can 'rebel against the tyranny of the selfish genes' within, and so manage to stay moderately nice even although programmed to be nasty. But this language is very unfortunate. Like all other living things, we have genes. We also have psychologies; that is, in accordance with our genetic recipes, and the environment in which these genes are turned into proteins and cells, brains have formed, so that we think and desire and talk and adapt ourselves to the culture around us. But what sense can we make of rebelling against this tyranny? Perhaps Dawkins has in mind an occasion when I really want to do something selfish, but control myself and do something nice for someone else instead. Why describe this as a case of defying my genes? It is only if we are in the grip of the idea of a ghost in the machine that we might oppose what 'nature' would have me do against what I, the real me, does. And that is wrong, because the real, biological, me is not a creature rebelling against the tyranny of his brain. The fact is that I am just using it. In the next chapter, we see more of this essentially bankrupt idea of the 'self' as an agent standing outside nature but mysteriously able to intervene in it.

Dawkins himself defines core Darwinism with wonderful concision and accuracy, as the view 'that evolution is guided in adaptively non-random directions by the non-random survival of small random hereditary changes.' The small changes happen in the genes, which then replicate, and the non-random survival rates are an index of the relative fitness of genes and alleles in their particular environments. But from the fact that an organism is of a type that has had to survive and to evolve, we cannot at all deduce that it has to care about nothing but its own survival, or its own 'interest', or the number of its own progeny, or their fecundity or any other single thing. The inference from function to overt psychology is simply fallacious. It is exactly like inferring from the fact that our sexual drives have an evolutionary function, namely procreation, that all we want when we want sex is to have children. Happily for human pleasures, and for the pharmacology industry, this is not so.

Nice guys finish . . . where?

Hence, for all Darwin tells us, we might take pleasure in helping others, in just the same spirit as we take pleasure in non-procreative sex. And there are plenty of evolutionary dynamics in which individuals who bear the cost of assisting their kin, those who have helped them, their neighbours or the collective, do better than those who do not. Nice guys sometimes do finish first, and this should be no more surprising than that less lethal parasites flourish rather than their greedier, but lethal, cousins – the dynamic whereby diseases such as myxomatosis in rabbits tend to become less lethal over time. By the same mechanism, in a world in which we must all hang together or else we all hang separately, those who are adapted to hang together do best (see *Is There Such a Thing as Society?*).

The sciences of the brain are indeed poised to tell us a great deal about ourselves. The neural mechanisms underlying emotion, happiness, other moods, and arousals and excitements are all proper subjects of intensive study. Will these studies answer the perennial questions of human nature? There is a more general difficulty.

Let us remember the question raised when we discussed my pleasurable daydream of the boulevards of Paris (see *Am I a Ghost in a Machine?*). The only correlation, if one can be found, between a particular fragment of the brain and my daydream of the boulevards is that if the fragment is altered or destroyed, perhaps my daydream changes or vanishes, or if the fragment is stimulated artificially, I begin dreaming of Paris again. Perhaps at a very high magnification, it is found that if this neuron is made to fire, then in my thoughts the sun comes out in Paris. That would be interesting, certainly, although in practice such highly localized causal powers seem not to be common (generally, more 'distributed' results occur in which whole neural networks are involved even in a distinct particular thought). But in any case, before a result like this affects how we think about human nature, we need to reflect that the psychology did not come out of the result, but went into it. The interpretation that this fragment of the brain is responsible for thinking about the boulevards of Paris is completely dependent on prior knowledge that the subject is indeed so thinking.

It is the subject's sayings and doings, the large-scale behaviour that falls under the common gaze, that enables us to judge how he or she is feeling or thinking. Even in ideal science, facts about the brain can only be interpreted psychologically by being calibrated against outward, observable sayings or doings or writings. To put it rather succinctly: brain writing needs calibrating against real writing.

This is fine for some purposes. But if the common behaviour of people leaves interpretation indeterminate or contested (as with questions like whether we are all selfish), the neurophysiology cannot by itself provide any help. In particular cases, indeed, brain events might play a subsidiary role. If someone apparently sincerely denies that he is angry, a quick scan might show brain activities that have in other cases been reliably correlated with anger, and this should make us more inclined to doubt his word. But if his behaviour is sufficiently calm, and his smiles look genuine and his voice sounds relaxed, then we just have one regularity about the brain at odds with others about the ways anger is manifested, and we may be in doubt as to what to think; while if there are not these other signs, then perhaps we could have told he was angry by ordinary observation. Just think how quick we are to notice the stress in someone's voice, the shiftiness in their eye, the false smile or the failure to suppress the flash of irritation.

A brave new future?

Questions about our real motives and real beliefs appear intractable because we would like generalizations and laws of behaviour, yet only find variation between individuals, change within individuals, and sometimes nice and sometimes nasty surprises. There are also persistent indeterminacies of interpretation. Did George save the drowning child because of sympathy or because he was hoping for glory? Does Betty bat her eyelashes at Albert because she loves him so, or because she wants to get stuff out of him? Sometimes we think we know, but often we cannot tell, and perhaps the subject cannot tell either, since our own capacity to interpret our own doings is far from perfect (see *How Can I Lie to Myself?*). Sometimes, perhaps, there is no fact of the matter. Betty may not know her own mind, and perhaps God could not either, because she is not single-minded when it comes to Albert, his love and his stuff.

There is clearly an urgent question about whether we can and should change human nature in the light of whatever science tells us about the mechanisms underlying our psychologies. A rather blunt response is that we already do, one person at a time. We do it when we socialize our children, when we teach them our language, when we introduce them to property and promises, forbearances and cooperations, conventions and norms, and the millions of little capacities that eventually fit them for their lives as grown-ups. This is an agonizing process, as parents know, and of course we endlessly debate and tinker with the choices in front of educators. We do not even know the best way to teach children to read, for example, and of course there may be no such thing as the best way: only a multitude of ways, some more suitable for some, and others for others.

That is cultural influence. But presumably, as eugenicists hoped, selective breeding, or genetic engineering, might in principle eventually change the gene pool and lead to different kinds of people.

Few people would quarrel with elimination or suppression of physical disease and illness to which some simple genetic peculiarity makes some people prone: Huntington's chorea and Duchenne's muscular dystrophy being perhaps the best publicly known examples. The question is whether we can imagine a genetic engineering, not to remove deficits and disease, but to improve human nature, rather as eugenic programmes were hoped to do around a century ago. We could imagine enhancements, producing people who are, for instance, more just, less selfish, more courageous, more intelligent, more imaginative, more prudent, more humorous and better company. Of course the aims of old eugenic programmes might strike us as comical when they were not wicked, but I am sure that today many people congratulate themselves on being able to do better. They, in the old days, ushered in a nightmare, but we, in the 21st century, will wave a wand. We know how to aim at utopia, and we are responsible enough to do so.

I do not think we should allow this optimism. First of all, there are obvious reasons for scientific caution. There are very few aspects of normal human development, and especially brain development, that are not polygenic, that is, dependent on a whole host of genes. So we immediately face a combinatorial explosion: if each of our 25,000 or so genes can interact in a great number of ways with even a small proportion of the remaining 24,999, the underlying processes may number in the millions, and the prospect of understanding them in fine detail is proportionately remote. The project of unravelling the genome itself, so widely applauded and heralded as ushering in the brave new dawn, was obviously trivial by comparison.

We would also be naive if we thought a genetic utopianism would be immune to the normal pressures of politics and commerce. The eugenicists of the 20th century were, for instance, Aryan racial supremacists, and had a very peculiar view of human excellence. Who would like to guess what those of this and subsequent centuries might be? Capitalism would like an intervention that promotes consumer envy and lifestyle discontent. People on the right would like one that diminishes concern for social justice, while those on the left would like one that increases it. Pharmaceutical companies would not pay for research to make childhood naughtiness disappear without their continued help, and while moralists put in their bid for kindness and intelligence, the Pentagon will press for a less compassionate and more obedient soldiery. In other words, we must beware of the idea that there is an abstraction called 'Science', an insightful, imaginative, impersonal, just, benevolent, invisible hand, and that we can leave the people of the future to it. There is no such hand.

Apart from scientific and political complexities, there are more philosophical problems. There are two resources coming from ancient philosophy that are relevant. One is the Socratic doctrine of the unity of the virtues: the idea that one cannot simply be courageous, or just, or generous, or merciful *tout court*. Exercising one virtue requires exercising others. If courage is not to be mere stupidity or mere lack of imagination, for example, it needs to be accompanied by awareness and judgement; equally, if it is not to go over the top into mad rashness, then it has to be combined with caution and prudence. Similarly for other virtues. A judge cannot be merciful without being courageous, since sometimes courage will be required in the face of the anger of people clamouring for punishment and death. And so on across the board.

This alone makes any project of 'improving' human nature with genetic intervention highly fraught. Do you want kinder, more generous people? We try to get them by bringing people up in kind environments, gently rewarding exhibitions of kindness, discouraging the reverse. But might we have a magic genetic bullet, bypassing this troublesome cultural exercise? Well, misjudged kindness is a bad thing: kind parents often spoil their children. They may smother them, patronize them, take away their initiative, infantilize them or prevent their maturity. As Aristotle said, we want a mean, and as the Socratic doctrine says, it must go along with judgement, tact, imagination, respect for the dignity of others and a host of other nuanced skills. Even then there will be little consensus on when just the right mean has been achieved. All we can do is aim in general directions, and then keep our fingers crossed.

The second point also emphasized in the classical tradition is that in the world as we have it, things become yet harder. Most people are generous some of the time: famously, Hitler was kind to animals. Suppose we found a genetic intervention that prevented the development of unkindness in any circumstance. This might seem to be a breakthrough, until we ask whether it also suppresses envy, jealousy, resentment and ambition, let alone justice – just some of the traits that have us being rather less generously disposed to some people than others. It seems that it must do so, but then is the resulting subject alert and spry, well adapted for enterprises and for the variety of tasks the human being may face? Or is he or she a kind of Stepford zombie, a lobotomized parody of anything we admire? Of course what we would like is someone who is kind and generous to the right degree in the right circumstances. We want what we already have, namely a relatively plastic disposition ready to be tuned by education and experience. But successfully navigating life's problems without experience is no more likely than speaking French without experience or navigating an unfamiliar city or coastline without experience.

Even if we confine ourselves to that old and apparently uncontroversial aim of eugenics, namely 'improved intelligence', worries arise. Intelligence can famously be used for good or bad, strategically or cooperatively. Wily Odysseus was the most intelligent of Agamemnon's men, much admired for his deceptions and frauds, lies and plots. And intelligence is not a monolithic trait. The charmed meadows of academic life are full of brilliant people in their field whom we would not trust very far outside it. Until researchers find a gene for getting hold of the wrong end of the stick, and manage to remove it from the population without any other side-effects, I think we should not hold our breath.

The investigation of human nature is, as I began by saying, as old as philosophy. It is as old as Homer and St Augustine, Shakespeare and Proust, and as new as the latest ideas from game theorists, evolutionary psychologists, neurophysiologists, pharmacologists, zoologists, economists and perhaps even quantum theorists and engineers. It is hard work listening to everyone, and we need to be careful. But we also need to be grateful for the feast.

Am I Free?
Choices and responsibility

The problem with free will is easily felt. Perhaps the world is a deterministic system. This means that its state at any time is controlled by its state at some earlier time, and so on back for ever. 'Control' here means that given the laws of nature, and given the earlier state, the later state follows by necessity.

It is as inexorable as the fact that if you are held under water you will drown, or if you jump out of a window you will fall. And then we seem to be helpless prisoners of events, and indeed of events stretching far back before our birth, to the beginning of time itself.

A dilemma

A different option is that there are elements of randomness within the system: sudden fits and starts, unpredictable in advance. Some people advocate this because quantum theory posits random events at the subatomic level, although whether this translates into randomness at the aggregate level is not obvious. Well, suppose we are blessed or cursed with random happenings, perhaps at the quantum level inside our brain, which are then amplified into random motions or thoughts or

choices. The trouble is that this is not what we wanted. We do
not regain responsibility by having an onboard roulette wheel
whose results then put events into motion. If the wheel is an
indeterministic system, then I can't be responsible for how it
finishes up – nothing can.

So the dilemma is that either nature is deterministic, which
removes any room for free will, or nature at best contains elements of randomness, which also removes any room for free will.

A blind alley

Faced with this dilemma, we might look for a notion of what we
are like that enables us to escape the problem. The image might
become one of the subject, the active person, deciding and
choosing in complete independence of the causally connected
events that make up physical nature. On this conception, it
would be as if the subject stands outside nature, in some kind of
vacuum beyond the reach of chemistry or physics, but then from
that uncontaminated vantage point can decide to step in to make
things happen, to twirl the knobs one way or the other. Some
have thought that our ordinary self-awareness discloses some
kind of 'unfettered' freedom, a kind of time-out from the usual
march of cause and effect. They say that this is what it feels like
to be a free agent, for we are often conscious of the free space in
which we can do what we like. I call this an interventionist conception of freedom: the free subject intervenes in the ongoing
course of the world, but is herself not caused to do so one way or
the other by events in that course.

There are many things wrong with this conception of

freedom. If it is what we require for freedom, then we cannot have any. First, it is incompatible with what we take ourselves to know about nature. Physical nature is a causally closed system: it takes a physical event and a physical force to make things happen, and those things include the chemical and electrical changes in the brain necessary for speech or action. And physical events do not float free of the ongoing course of nature – on the contrary, nature is constituted entirely by them.

Suppose we put this objection aside, perhaps clinging on to the dualist picture of a 'soul' or 'self' somehow lodged in the system of brain and body which otherwise seems to make us up: a ghost lodged in the machine which is our physical embodiment. The problem then is to understand how our physical world, including information in the form of electrical currents, excitations of the brain, stored memories and the rest of our cognitive equipment, actually interacts with the ghost inside. There has to be a two-way interaction. There must be events that influence the choosing agent. We do not issue choices in an informational vacuum, but in the light of information about the environment within which we are to act. Perhaps when that information has arrived, there is still the executive choice, and it is here that freedom holds sway. But the ghost in turn must not only bring about ghostly events. It must roll its sleeves up and make things happen in the physical world. So the full picture is that nature presents its energies to the ghost, and the ghost then pushes the chemical and physical brain about, altering its course of action. Not only is this unbelievable, but it only postpones the problem of free will. For how does the ghost make its decisions? Is it a determinate system, with a nature of its own? Or is it prone to random fits and starts? Either way there is the same dilemma afflicting the ghost that was supposed to afflict us: is it determined or is it random? Adding an internal ghost does not escape the dilemma that either way free will seems to vanish.

What we are aware of, and how we act

I said that for some people this picture of ourselves as ghosts in a machine is encouraged by 'what it feels like' to make a free choice. But is it? It is certainly true that as we choose we are not conscious of the multiple processes that sustain our mental states. We are not gifted with an awareness of what is going on in our brains, for instance, or many of our muscles. When we smile at something, for example, we are attending to whatever we smile at. We are completely unconscious of the many muscular and neurological processes that are needed to enable us to smile. But that just means we are not conscious of such processes. It does not mean that we are conscious of there being no such processes. If there were no such processes, we would not be able to smile, nor be able to decide to smile either. This means that there is no such thing as 'consciousness of freedom'. All that we are conscious of is the world on which we decide to act and then, if things go well, our own acting.

If our awareness of decision-making does not support it, then we can abandon the interventionist conception of free will in favour of a more realistic model. We need one that can be reconciled to what we know about the way of the world. The solution is to see the human being, you and me, not as an alien intruder into the world of nature, but as part of it: a complicated part, indeed, but subject to just the same laws and processes as many other parts. We have systems that take in information (the senses), that process it (our cognitive systems), that integrate it with stored memories, that then attach emotional temperature and direction to it, in the shape of desires or aversions, and that issue in impulses to the motor cortex initiating choice and action. The aggregate of these systems, when things go well, is a responsible person, in control of their doings, and responsible for them if their choices are rash or negligent or otherwise defective.

So what does our freedom consist in? In a word, in our responsiveness to reasons. Reasons are facts about the situation that we are in, and facts that suggest or require appropriate responses. We are responsive to reasons in a similar way to that in which a thermostat is responsive to ambient temperature. But unlike the thermostat, we are multi-dimensional. The situations in which we act are not characterized by one variable – temperature – but by many. We put together complex pictures of complex situations, perhaps ones with some factors pulling one way, and others pulling another. The arts of judgement and practical wisdom consist in noticing the right things in the right way, and often take experience and practice, and perhaps a certain amount of luck.

This is all very well, you might say, but where in all this description of the decision-making agent does free will get in? Haven't we lost sight of the baby in the rush of bathwater? Suppose that Alfred's decision-making is really, really bad, the upshot of a malevolent or careless or forgetful or dogmatic character, while Betty is benevolent, careful, well-stocked with information which she easily accesses and properly open-minded. Betty does good things; Alfred messes things up. But why blame Alfred? He is not responsible for being the way he is – indeed, according to our original dilemma, the events responsible for that form a chain stretching way back into historical time, or even deep geological time. The humourist and philosopher Michael Frayn nicely expresses the sense of loss here:

> A sovereign of the old school I had always felt myself to be, benevolent but absolute, the source of all the edicts that constitute the fabric of the court and its business, the master of my own revels. Now it has pleased me to command this inquiry into my own authority, however, I discover that I am not an absolute ruler after all. I am a mere constitutional fiction, a face on the postage stamps, a signature at the bottom of degrees written by unidentified powers behind the throne over which I have no control . . . even my private entertainments are devised for me by invisible courtiers working in parts of the palace that I have never entered, and could never find my way to.

We do not blame Alfred for drowning if he is held under water. So why blame him for the bad decisions that an unkind fate has determined his systems to land on? Isn't he just a victim or a patient, like the powerless constitutional monarch in titular control of a court whose doings are in fact determined by unidentified powers behind the throne?

If we let these questions overwhelm us we will either be driven back to the incoherent interventionist conception of freedom, or become sceptical about the whole notion. But the questions should not overwhelm us. For it is not 'powers behind the throne' that make Alfred do as he does. It is the powers that constitute the throne – in other words, the systems that make up the person he is.

The responsible thermostat

We must build up our conception of Alfred's being responsible for what he does by thinking again of simpler systems. The thermostat in my house is responsible for the ambient temperature. That is what it controls. It does not control the temperature in your house. If it goes wrong, its defect is responsible for the temperature going awry, and I may have to repair it or get rid of it and substitute a new one. The thermostat cannot be defended on the ground that it did not control the way it was made. That is no doubt true, but not to the point. It still controlled the temperature, only it did it badly. It is being blamed for the temperature, not for its own construction (a different machine may be to blame for that).

I cannot improve the thermostat by arguing with it, and I cannot motivate it to behave better by the threat of penalties or the promise of rewards. That is because the thermostat is a simple, one-dimensional mechanism. But human beings can be motivated by threats and rewards. We are responsive not only to overt input from other people, but to what we rehearse in our imaginations. The very idea of being seen doing something may be enough to change our behaviour (see *Why Be Good?* and *Do We Need God?*). So our social world is built partly out of nudges and corrections, frowns and smiles, admiration and disapproval.

If I get angry at you for a piece of bad behaviour, I am simply playing a part in that social world. If you protest at my anger, I will cite the reasons why you should have behaved better; if these reasons did not occur to you, or occurred to you and did not sway you, then that was a fault in you. Like the thermostat, you may need to be repaired, if we know how, or replaced, if we can do so. My anger is a reaction to what you did, but it also has a function. It signals a kind of rejection, and this may give you pause if you are tempted to repeat your delinquency, or may give others pause if they are tempted to imitate you.

When do we decide?

In recent years neurophysiological results have been pressed into the free will debate. In particular the neurologist Benjamin Libet discovered facts about the timing of actions that were sometimes interpreted as casting doubt on free will. By making measurements of the electrical activity in the motor cortex, or part of the brain involved in the initiation of action, Libet discovered an increase of 'readiness potential' for an action, measurable around one-third of a second before the subject's conscious decision to move. The subject would report deciding to press a button at one time, but the electrical measurement showed that the neurological events setting the action in train were already under way before the time to which the subject referred their decision. It seemed to many that this showed that it is not our own acts of will that cause our actions, but unconscious processes, powers behind the throne as it were, preceding our conscious decisions.

This interpretation of Libet's result is not, however, forced on us. Indeed, it only seems plausible if we surreptitiously hark back to the model of the ghost in the machine. Our self-report is then thought of as a reliable report of when the ghost stirred itself, but the preceding readiness potential shows that the machine was stirring itself before that, so alas and alack, the ghost did not make anything happen after all! But if we avoid thinking like that, we can take a very different view of the results. What we have is that the time to which the subject refers the decision is a little later than the time at which the motor cortex is active in implementing it. But there is no reason to say that we actually do take decisions at the time to which we refer them, or the time at which we become conscious of them.

Consider the familiar situation of lying in bed on a cold morning, vaguely aware that you ought to be getting up. You sort of make an effort, but lie back. Perhaps you do it again. And then one time, you find yourself up. That was the time you finally decided to get up. It should not be in the least surprising that the motor processes surrounding that occasion were different, and perhaps becoming different, in ways completely unknown to you yet preceding the time you thought you decided. That was the occasion on which you succeeded in getting up, and no doubt there were things, about which you know nothing, making you succeed then when you had failed previously. It doesn't mean that you did not decide to get up. You did, and may be praised for it, just as if you had gone on lying in bed you might have been blamed for failing to do whatever you should have done that morning. Because we know nothing about what made that exercise of will successful when others had not been, it can feel as though 'I just found myself up and out of bed'. It is as if the

action came mysteriously from elsewhere (just as it often feels
as if our thoughts come mysteriously from elsewhere, sometimes
embarrassingly). To revert to Frayn's analogy, it is the whole
court who is deciding to get up: you, the sum total of your
systems. Not the 'sovereign' acting independently of his subordi-
nates, but the constitutional government as a whole.

The question of *when* you decided to get up conceals a con-
fusion, like the question, 'When did you win the race?' The
success happened as you breasted the tape before all the others.
But you were occupied in winning the race from the time you
started running. You cannot pooh-pooh a runner's achievement
by saying, 'Oh, winning races – that's easy. It only takes a milli-
second to do it.' Similarly you were occupied in deciding to get
up as you lay in bed feeling warm and lazy but aware all the time
that it had to happen soon. And then – bingo! You were up, perhaps to your surprise, just as at the end you may have won the
race, perhaps to your surprise.

So does the free will problem boil down to that old philosophical cliché that 'it all depends on what you mean by' free
will? If you want the sovereign independence of the uncaused
ghost, you cannot have it. If you are willing to settle for the constitutional government of a massive neurological and anatomical
system working in harmony and responsive to reasons, then you
can have it. I think that you ought to be willing to settle.

Sorry, it's your fault

Being responsive to reasons is the feature we actually do use to
attribute praise and blame, responsibility and control. In Eng-

lish law there used to be a rule for determining whether a crim-
inal was mentally ill, and therefore presumably less than fully
responsible for his crime. The question was 'whether he would
have done it with a policeman standing at his elbow'. The
rationale is that if he would not, then (a) presumably he knew
that what he was doing was wrong and (b) he was capable of
responding to incentives and disincentives – in this case the certainty of being caught. A plea for diminished responsibility
would succeed only if it was doubtful that even the policeman
would have deterred him.

I think that is a pretty good rule of thumb. But it may apply
more widely than in dramatic cases of mental incapacity. In
more humdrum circumstances people may be less responsive to
reasons than they should be. We talk of people being 'slaves of
fashion' or 'slaves to convention', where the image of slavery is
that they are in the grip of something: as a result of some experience or some (mis)education, the discomfort at not being
in fashion or not behaving conventionally overrides other
normal reasons. The slave of fashion may not steal clothes if a
policeman is at her elbow, but she may buy them even if bank-
ruptcy is. Addiction works by making us less responsive to
reasons than we should be, and we talk of people being unable to
help themselves, or even being out of control, and perhaps we
say that it is no good being angry with them. We turn instead to
supposing that they need treatment or therapy.

This may be wise in particular cases. But it is not wise across
the board. By insisting on seeing ourselves and others as responsible we maintain the practices of reason. We maintain the habit
of turning over in our own minds what to do, and what counts for

or against particular decisions. And we maintain our social world, in which reactive emotions such as anger, or disappointment, or even contempt stand alongside patience, encouragement, admiration and praise as part of the endless adjustments we each need to make to the many ways in which our lives interact with those of others. None of our actual practices require contra-causal, ghostly freedom. All that they require is that we do not regard ourselves and others as zombies, or, if we are serious pessimists about the human condition, at any rate that we try not to do so more often than we deserve.

What Do We know?
Virtual realities and valuable authorities

What do you know? You know a great deal, actually. My bet is that you, like me, know your own name and those of your parents. You are likely to know whether you are lying down or not, which country you are in, who is the current President of the United States, and a great many other things of that kind.

You know how to peel a banana, what it will taste like, and unless you have been living it up a bit too much – in which case you know what it is like to feel under the weather – you know where you were last night. You know a lot about what you can and cannot do, and a fair bit about how to make things happen: how to get at the contents of a tin or make a cup of coffee. You also know a fair bit about what you do not know: you know that you do not know how to speak quite a lot of languages, and probably do not know how to operate a nuclear submarine. Some things that you do not know, you know how to find out. If you do not know what is in the store cupboard you can open it and look. If you do not know someone's email address you can probably google them and find it, or just ask someone. These unpretentious things are givens, fixed in your life and in all your calculations about what to do.

The sceptic

All this may make it a little surprising how much philosophical
attention has been paid to the figure of the sceptic, the imaginary opponent who casts doubt far and wide, issuing wholesale
dismissals of claims to knowledge. Many people come to
philosophy by first reading the *Meditations* of René Descartes, a
book structured around Descartes's wrestling with the thought
that perhaps all his experience is delusory, that he inhabits a virtual reality, with all his experiences and thoughts fed into him
by a *malin génie*, or evil demon, bent on deceiving him. Similar
thought experiments inform popular movies like *The Matrix*.
The idea of a virtual reality is common enough, so how am I to
show that I do not inhabit one? I might be a brain in a vat with
a mad scientist pumping delusory experiences into me, and
everything might be a dream, after all. So perhaps I surreptitiously made it easy to sprinkle knowledge claims around by
casting the question in the title plural and not the singular: 'What
do we know?' as opposed to the more solipsistic question, 'What
do I know?' Descartes posed his problem to himself, alone with
his thoughts.

Even lonely sceptical thoughts have a short shelf life. As soon
as we give ourselves a shake and walk out of our studies, they
evaporate. Out in the street, we may meet people who ask us if
we know the way to such-and-such a place, but we do not meet
people who ask if we know we are in a street. But sceptical
thoughts intrigue philosophers in spite of that. Partly it would be
nice to be able to defeat them: it would be nice to have proof that
I am not in fact in a virtual reality. So that is a possible philo-

sophical ambition. But I am going to ignore it, for the moment, and return to the public question, leaving the more radical total scepticisms until later.

Day-to-day knowledge and Potemkin barns

The public question can give us urgent political and economic problems. When people ask, for instance, whether economics or psychoanalysis is a science, what they are really interested in is whether economic predictions or psychoanalytic interpretations of personality are soundly based. Are they based on knowledge of how economies or psychologies work? Or are they speculative and based on mere cobwebs of theory? These are not idle questions: they determine who get the highly paid jobs and consultancies, and where human efforts get spent. But without at least the glimmering of an epistemology – a story about the structure of knowledge and its scope and limits – they cannot be tackled.

Again, courts may need to determine whether 'creationist science' is a science and that its theories therefore deserve airing in schools, and that too requires ascertaining whether there is anything like knowledge in the area of evolutionary history and orthodox biology. So epistemology matters.

Plato is credited with offering the first account of what we mean by knowledge, which was in three parts: you know something, he thought, if you hold it to be true, if it is true and if you are justified in holding it to be true. Why the third condition? Why not hold that you know something if you hold it to be true, and you are right to do so? Plato's answer was that you might be right just by luck or chance, and that is not good enough. But this in turn raises tricky questions. First of all, you might be right by luck or chance but still know something. For it may be by luck or chance that you came to know the truth: you just happened to be in the right place at the right time. On the other hand, you might be justified in believing something which is perfectly true, but still only be right by luck or chance.

Thus suppose you see a barn by the roadside and believe it to be a barn. Perfectly justifiable, since you can usually tell when you are looking at a barn. But unknown to you, you have driven into a land of 'Potemkin barns': fake barn façades put up by Hollywood studios. (Grigori Potemkin was a minister of Catherine the Great of Russia, and is supposed to have deceived her about the value of his conquests in the Crimea by erecting false façades of villages when she went on tour, so all looked rosy.) By chance you happened to have looked at one of the rare real barns, so while your belief was justified and true, you didn't really know you were looking at a barn. This last kind of example was first brought to philosophical prominence by Edmund Gettier, and caused a huge amount of discussion about the relationship between reliability, justification, and the question of whether your belief was in some sense causally responsive to the facts in the right way. Whole careers have been spent toiling in what became known as the Gettier salt mines.

To clear the decks, it is best to think of our purpose in building a notion of knowledge in the first place. Suppose we are in simple circumstances, perhaps back in the Stone Age. It would be desirable to be sure where the tiger is. Suppose a tribesperson, Ug, says where it is. We want to be confident enough to accept Ug's word for it. So we want reliability from Ug. This in turn means Ug should be in a better position than guessing: this is what was right about Plato's original idea. Ug should have done things that make him a good informant, and we probably have a good idea about what those are. He should have looked, and have seen or heard strong signs of the position of the tiger. These signs in turn will be things that would not have been as they are had the tiger not been where Ug thinks. This is what we need, as persons being informed by Ug. In turn Ug himself needs awareness of what he has seen and done, and of the fact that what he has seen or done is a good indication of the whereabouts of the tiger.

Grading information

What we require of the informant is some property or other that makes him the person whose word we should accept. I do not think we are actually particularly choosy about what this property is. After all, our primary concern is the whereabouts of the tiger, not how Ug came to know it. He may have consulted the oracle, or the idea may have just popped into his head unbidden, or he may have in turn been told; he may have smelled, seen or heard the tiger. It does not matter, provided that when he consults the oracle or when ideas pop into his head he tends to be right, just as when he smells, sees or hears the tiger. Of course, in the actual world, we are wise to prefer the last three. But in some cases people know the answer without being able at all to say how they know it. This is the position of most of us when it comes to recognizing faces, for example. And in principle an oracle might be reliable, just as some people who tell us things are.

When Ug tells the whereabouts of the tiger, he may be challenged. How does he know where it is? This is an important
question, since our choices and our lives may hang on whether
he indeed knows what he claims to know. If his answer is flimsy
or evasive or unconvincing, we still can't be sure where the tiger
is. We need to know whether would-be informants have done
their stuff properly. We learn, when we are very young, the
uncomfortable truth that not everybody can be trusted on everything, and that some people can be trusted on practically
nothing. We need practice and skill at sorting the good from the
bad. The verdict that someone knows where the tiger is, or that
I myself know where the tiger is, is a verdict on what to trust.

So challenges in practice tend to be highly specific. It is
whether someone in a particular context, making a particular
claim, is to be believed or not. Challenges ask whether some possibility or other has in fact been ruled out by the informant's
evidence (or by our own evidence, if we are interrogating our
own position, as we often do). In everyday life many possibilities
are merely bare possibilities, too far-fetched to bother with. This
is sometimes a matter of experience and judgement. Visual hal-
lucinations are possible, but in the street the sight of a bus
bearing down on me leaves me no time nor inclination to consider the question of whether it is a relevant possibility. Bare
possibilities are properly ignored. Real possibilities, on the other
hand, defeat claims to know. If Ug's evidence (say, old droppings)
leave a real possibility that the tiger is somewhere other than
where he found them (tigers do move about), then Ug is not to
be listened to; he does not know what he claimed to know.

Experience and justification

Is a philosopher such as Descartes at fault for treating as real possibilities what are in truth only bare possibilities? He indeed does this, but I do not think he is at fault, for whether a possibility is relevant may vary with the context. For practical purposes we ignore many possibilities which for theoretical purposes we might wish to consider (time reversal, zombies, unwitnessed scenes, the failure of laws of nature, time travel, are just some of those in this book). The theoretical purpose is not usually to cast doubt on our knowledge, but to force us to puzzle over how our sensory information, information-processing facilities, memories and other cognitive faculties work to enable us to know as much as we do.

Our knowledge of the empirical world starts with the way in which sensory experience is transmuted into confidence in particular propositions. It easily does so: seeing a red barn, I make no doubt about judging, instantly, that this is indeed what it is. But there is a step here, as we can see if we take something at which we are less good. Seeing a magenta barn, I may not know what colour it is, since I am not perfectly certain which hues count as magenta. Hearing a note on the piano and having poor pitch, I cannot tell at all which note it is. Perhaps the process is purely causal: some sights cause me to judge, reliably and truly, that things are one way or the other. Whereas hearing a note unfortunately does not cause me to judge with any reliability which note it is, although it may cause you to do so.

Some philosophers have resisted the idea that there is a purely causal process here. They insist that the relation between experience and judgement has to be one of *justification*. Purely causal processes, they say, do not justify us in believing anything as a result of them. Being hit on the head may cause me to believe I am on the moon, but cannot justify that belief. And after all, our experiences are frequently the terminus of justification. We want 'I saw him' to explain why I believe that the robber was Jesse James, but also to justify me in claiming that it was. But my own view is that we have to be more careful. 'I heard it' does not justify my claim that the note was middle C if I have imperfect pitch. It is only if I am well prepared or attuned, or in other words if the right causal stimulus in experience reliably sets me judging rightly how things stand, that my judgement is worth anything. I am only justified in believing that my glimpse was of some celebrity if I am good at recognizing the celebrity in question, and that can of course be separately tested, as it would be in an identity parade. It is only if I have some reason to believe that an instrument like a voltmeter is reliable, giving results that co-vary causally with the rise and falls of voltage, that I can trust its readings. Similarly it is only after I have become a well-calibrated instrument, that is, I have learned to interpret my experience reliably, that I can stop the question of how I know by saying that I saw or heard something.

It is an interesting question whether experience itself should be thought of as ready interpreted, pre-cooked for us, as it were. Most philosophers think it should. Clearly experience conditions experience: the ear hears a surrounding language differently after it is familiar and understood than when it is new and a mere babble, and the same is true for other senses. But as far as the theory of knowledge goes, it makes little difference whether interpretation is done unconsciously, before experience comes into our minds, or consciously, afterwards. It had still better be a reliable process.

Flaws and failures

I may be normally pretty reliable, but become much less so when other mental states get involved. People are less reliable when their emotions run high, when they are subject to misleading cues, unusual conditions, distractions or external pressure. Beliefs are contagious, and eyewitnesses, however confident, may interpret what they saw in the light of what others told them they saw. And we tend to think we are more reliable, and across wider fields of judgement, than we are. Sometimes we have to discount even very immediate interpretations of experience: at a conjuring show our eyes may be telling us that we saw a man draw an egg out of his ear, but we are unwise to believe them. We bring in our knowledge of the way of the world to discount even what our eyes are telling us. Experience is the routine foundation of our beliefs, but sometimes has to give way to general knowledge which, in turn, will have been forged through a longer course of experience.

Once an epistemology has given us some sense of our footing in experience, it would be nice if there were a unique, authoritative, truth-delivery system enabling us to erect more ambitious generalizations and theories, explanations and predictions on its basis. After all, we do not simply catalogue the world one frame at a time, as it were. We generalize and predict, and this enables us to control our lives and organize our responses and plans.

Unfortunately philosophers have managed to find very few rules of method beyond some fairly trivial platitudes. We must not leap to conclusions too quickly, nor be too slow to recognize what are evidently the best explanations of the things we know. We have to test and experiment, and interpretations of tests and experiments are in turn contestable in the light of yet further evidence. The higher our ambitions, the greater the chance of a fall: we are more likely to be wrong making daring generalizations than when confining our attention to the routine and the familiar. There are very few codifiable rules for good sense and wise judgement, which is why programming computers to cope with anything more than very circumscribed environments proves so difficult (see *Can Machines Think?*).

One of the most influential views of our situation as theorists is that of Karl Popper, famous for his delineation of scientific method as that of bold conjectures, followed by severe testing. The theories that emerge are those that have survived in a kind of Darwinian process that weeds out competing theories. Popper himself had no very satisfactory theory of testing: at some points he seemed to think it was a conventional matter whether you described a test as having refuted a theory at all. This was a consequence of another aspect of his view, which was that nobody could ever be justified in holding a theory other than provisionally, on hold as it were for yet more testing. The first major problem is that if this is so, then we become equally unjustified in being sure that a test of the appropriate type was performed, had the results reported, or would have been likely to falsify the theory in question in any case. Testing is itself a theory-laden activity, requiring all kinds of confidence. (This is more obviously so in advanced sciences, where testing is conducted by extremely sophisticated instruments, whose behaviour is only given by extremely sophisticated theories.)

Another major problem is that unless survival in Popper's Darwinian process is allowed to increase our confidence in theories, then we never seem able to rely on them with the confidence that we do. It is all very well saying that it is a bold unfalsified conjecture that my GPS will tell me where I am. But unless it is a bold conjecture I can rely upon, that gives me no reason to spend any money on it. The cavemen would not go out of their way to avoid the thicket if it was just a bold unfalsified conjecture that Ug told them the tiger was there because he saw it. I do not want it to be a bold conjecture that my flight will lift off and answer to the controls. I want it to be a racing certainty. For that we need our confidence to match what happens. That is the gold standard, for knowledge and truth alike.

This also casts a better light on whether a subject like economics is a science. Economics issues plenty of bold, testable predictions about what is going to happen. But so do oracles (unless, like the oracle at Delphi, they give notoriously evasive answers). From the sidelines the trouble seems to be that they are mostly wrong.

So in the light of all this how do we cope with the nightmare of total scepticism? Might I be alone in my dream? No. It is a bare, outlandish possibility. If it is a possibility at all, it is certainly rightly ignored for most of our lives. If I cannot rule it out, that is only because it *allows me nowhere to stand* in order to start ruling it out. It is one of those tricksy questions that seems reasonable, but that conceals the seeds of its own unanswerable

nature that it nevertheless contains. It contains them, because as
soon as we start advancing things that give reasons for ruling it
out, the sceptic trains his 'How do you know?' on those things,
and so on forever. If we decline to get into the game, then lots of
things rule it out: the solid ground beneath my feet shows I am
not dreaming, and other people's sayings and doings show that
I am not alone in that dream.

Are We Rational Animals?
Reason in theory and practice

'What a piece of work is a man, how noble in reason, how infinite in faculties, in form and moving how express and admirable, in action how like an angel, in apprehension how like a god!' says Hamlet. His selection of reason as an especial mark of nobility, and of apprehension as almost divine, has met with wide approval from philosophers.

From Plato and Aristotle onwards, our capacities for reason have been seen as the crowning glory of humanity: the bit that sets us apart from other, 'lower' animals, and is even a special mark of divine favour.

Some shadows

There are two broad categories of reason. The first gives us theoretical reason, and the second practical reason. We use theoretical reason to adjust our beliefs and actions to the world. Its business is cognition, or the knowledge of how things stand. Practical reason, on the other hand, is for selecting actions: adjusting what we do in the light of that cognition, and in the light of our concerns or desires. Theoretical reason is then comparable to the navigator's map, which brings him the lie of the land, but does not tell him where to go. It is our concerns and desires that set us on one course or another.

Some sceptics have doubted whether theoretical reason is all that it is cracked up to be. When apparently powerful trains of reasoning lead to unwanted consequences, it may be convenient to revoke the triple A rating that reason might otherwise command. Thus religious apologists, under attack for promoting views which seem quite beyond, or contrary to, any that reason can justify, may retort by denying that reason is all that trustworthy a faculty. Indeed, it may be a merit, in their eyes, to manage to have faith in certain things that it is quite unreasonable to believe. Others, including David Hume, have argued that when we reason about reasonings we are led to pessimism and despair about our powers of sifting truth from falsehood, or getting any transparent view of how things stand.

Other sceptics have wondered quite what practical reason amounts to. Behaving reasonably may be contrasted favourably with behaving emotionally. But it is now more common to think that mechanisms of 'affect' or emotion underlie almost any decision, attaching a positive sign to some outcomes and a negative sign to others, thereby steering us a course. And the suggestion is that it is only emotion and desire, or what used to be called the 'passions', that do that.

A priori and a posteriori

The tradition divides theoretical reasonings into the 'a priori' and the 'a posteriori'. An inference is a priori if anyone who understands the issue must see that it holds. So, for example, it is a priori that if there are three people in the room, then there are more than two. Nobody who understands these claims could dissent, and we do not have to go and look to accept the conditional proposition (the if . . . then . . . claim). Logic and mathematics provide the central examples of a priori inferences: the inference from there being three to there being more than two is a modest but cast-iron mathematical inference, while if my friend is either in China or India, and I learn that he is not in China, logic enables me to infer that he is in India. By contrast, an inference is a posteriori if it depends on the way things are. In previous times, if someone travelled from London to New York, then they went by boat; more recently that has become an unreliable inference, since they are much more likely to have gone by air. A posteriori inferences show us deploying what we know or believe about the way of the world, and in principle and in practice that can change.

The category of a priori reason provokes philosophical disquiet. We discover most things by using our senses, putting ourselves in a position to receive information about how things happen to stand. How can there be a class of inferences which we know to be sound without any help from experience? Perhaps we are hard-wired to make these inferences, and in that sense some basic logical or mathematical understanding is innate. But even if the tendency is innate, that does not imply that it is trustworthy, for might we not be 'programmed' to make mistakes or at best near misses? A different suggestion is that they are essentially trivial, matters of convention or perhaps of linguistic rules that we ourselves lay down, and then teach children with their native language. If a philosopher is puzzled that we can infer a

priori that when there are three things of a kind then there must
be more than two, we might reply that this is just the way the
mathematical language works. After all, nobody finds it mysterious that when today is Monday tomorrow must be Tuesday.
That is just how we carry out the naming of the days of the week.
It might then be interesting to understand why mathematics
works so well, but the fact that its rules are as they are would be
just 'down to us', like the days of the week, or the fact that the
king in chess is the piece that can be in check.

Although this conventionalism about the a priori has its par-
tisans, it can seem quite unrealistic. The a priori attracts
attention because it is inexorable. We might perhaps change the
language whereby we say it, or we might even lose interest in
saying it at all, but twist and turn how we will, seven plus five is
still going to be twelve. Conventions and the rules of games are
things we control, and can change; mathematics and logic are
like granite. Furthermore, it signals an intellectual earthquake
when a view that was previously held to be valid a priori becomes
doubtful. The shift when Euclidean geometry began to seem
contingent, so that we could no longer say from the armchair
that triangles in a plane must have angles adding up to two right
angles, was a major mathematical upheaval. It was a revolution
in physics when Einstein said that you could no longer infer,
from the fact that A truly judges two events to be simultaneous,
that if B judges them not to be he must be wrong. These
upheavals show something more than the 'mere' replacement of
one rule of language or convention by another.

In fact, they suggest a rather different line of thought, which
is that the category of a priori inference is unreliable, and that

rather than a hard and fast distinction, we just have degrees of centrality or degrees of attachment. On this account, the propositions and inferences we call a priori are just the ones we would be most reluctant to give up, or the ones it requires scientific genius, reacting to anomalies and stresses in overall scientific theory, to challenge. Rather than the a priori being the category of God-given unchallengeable truths, it becomes the category of things to which we happen to be most attached, or at least most attached at a particular time and place in the history of thought. It is difficult to 'think outside the box' of ordinary logic or mathematics, but then it was difficult to think outside the box of Euclidean geometry or the non-relativistic framework of space and time. But we flatter ourselves if we are confident that what we find difficult cannot possibly be correct. What we describe as 'self-evident' may just be what is evident to us, at a particular time, after our minds have been trained to a particular shape by teaching and repetition.

Forecasts

When we turn to a posteriori reasoning, the picture is one of even more fragile and temporary confidences and reliances. The big bad bug here is the way in which our sporadic and fitful experience, closely bounded within a narrow compass of space and time, somehow gives us confidence in wider, more general, or even boundless truths about the way things are. We see and experience a little of the world, for a few years, but we believe things about the laws of nature, the invariable patterns in which events fall out, and have fallen out, and will fall out. We may be

modest enough not to go in for some kinds of forecasting, such
as economic forecasting or even weather forecasting. But we are
entirely confident that the solar system will continue its revolutions, that gravity will hold, that bodies will cohere and not
spontaneously fly apart, that the bread that sustains us today will
do so tomorrow. In all of these cases our lives (like those of animals) seem to be premised on the view that what holds good
within our experience will hold good outside it, and holds good
elsewhere, and has held good since long before we came on the
scene. In other words, it is premised on the uniformity of nature
(see *Why Do Things Keep On Keeping On?*). More theoretical scientific reasonings imply confidence that our models of the way
things work are accurate, or that explanations that appeal to us as
simple or natural are likely to be true. These confidences determine what we call 'reasonable', but are they anything more than
brave but faltering steps into the unknown? And if so, does that
undermine their claim to adjudicate what it is reasonable to
believe?

Practical reasons

The other major domain where we like to talk about reason is in
connection with practical reason. This is reason not for belief,
but for action and feeling, emotion and attitude. The fact that it
is annoying his sister Ann is a reason for Brian to stop blowing
his trumpet. Ann's distress is a reason for Cicely to feel sympathy
for her. It would be reasonable for Brian's parents to intervene,
but not reasonable for them to punish Brian by locking him in
the coal cellar for the night. In saying such things we put forward

approvals and disapprovals of lines of conduct, choices and the various stances that people take towards things. We endorse, or criticize, each other's responses to practical situations. Our selection of reasons here manifests our practical stances, including moral and ethical stances.

It would be nice if these endorsements or criticisms themselves had the imprint of a universal shared faculty of unimpeachable authority: Reason itself, or Rationality, a common birthright of all human creatures. Unfortunately, and in spite of the hard work of generations of philosophers, there is little prospect of establishing that. Criticizing Brian as unreasonable is indeed criticizing him. But it is not much more than that, and, in particular, it is no kind of guide to just what is wrong with him. In this case he is insufficiently sensitive, we think, to Ann's annoyance at his trumpet playing. But Brian may not think that: he may think Ann is oversensitive, or that her distress is a ploy to cull sympathy from their parents, or dozens of other things. Some of these may themselves involve unreasonable beliefs, but not all of them. Brian may find it difficult to put himself in Ann's shoes not because he is unreasonable but because he lacks sufficient imagination – after all, he finds the noise of the trumpet magnificent – or sufficient sympathy for what it must feel like to have a trumpet-playing brother. In a nutshell, Brian's defects may lie more with his heart than with his head. He is not in the same plight as someone who contradicts themselves, or is totally out of touch with the way of the world. Indeed, he may be in no kind of plight at all. His selfishness or insensitivity or lack of imagination might stand him in good stead: sadly, fortune in many human endeavours, such as business or politics, seems to favour not so much the brave as the insensitive, pig-headed, selfish and unimaginative.

The lack of moorings that this train of thought suggests is highly disturbing. It undermines any classical notion of an established and knowable, authorized version of human thought and action, a transparent script for action which we have to follow. It replaces it with a vision of nothing but the 'arbitrary' clashes of preference and will, when some people feel one way and others, feeling a different way, express their hostility at them or disappointment in them. When David Hume, the first forceful exponent of this vision, said that 'reason is, and ought only to be the slave of the passions, and can never pretend to any other office than to serve and obey them,' he triggered all kinds of fears – nihilism, scepticism, relativism – and they have continued to haunt writers from Immanuel Kant, writing shortly afterwards, to today.

Kant's response was to attempt to show that there is a 'maxim', or small cluster of maxims, of action that must be accepted by any practical agent. A maxim is a principle of action such as 'Do as you would be done by' or 'Look for agreement.' The aim is to show that to flout or ignore some principle would forfeit something essential to the very idea of being an agent. Kant's own proposal is that it would be contrary to 'pure practical reason' to act on a principle if you could not, at the same time, will that everyone else act on it as well. There is something attractive about this, just as there is something unattractive about claiming exemptions for oneself from policies that one applies to others. There is something very off-colour about admitting that the state has to collect taxes from people, while avoiding them oneself, or being glad that most people most of the time are truthful, while oneself happily deceiving others whenever the occasion demands. Kant has at the least put his finger on something we expect of each other, and of good citizens in general.

However, there is room for doubt about the status of these good thoughts. Are they really certified by reason itself, or do they just represent the kinds of concern we expect of good citizens, or the kinds of concern we know to be necessary if the kind of life we like is to flourish? Perhaps the most compelling of Kantian examples is that of the lying promise. If I promise you to do something, knowing that I have no intention of complying, am I not acting in a way that I could not possibly want everyone to act? For if they did, the whole activity of giving and receiving promises with any meaning would crumble. If every 'promise' had as a get-out clause 'provided I feel like it', then no promise would be worth trusting, nor therefore worth voicing. I would regard this as catastrophic: a breakdown of all social bonds. Yet even here someone could feel differently. They might imagine some kind of golden age of free individuals unchained from the bonds of society, or they might imagine a self-reliant, glamorous life rather like that depicted in the Icelandic sagas, where binding laws and solemn promises of good behaviour seemed to mean almost nothing. I can certainly say that anyone is unreasonable to idealize or desire such an imagined state, but that just registers my fear of it or unease at the thought of it: in other words, not the deliverance of pure reason, but a contingent emotional distaste.

Then there are cases where individuals quite happily act in ways that not everyone can follow, yet are not irrational, and not

even at all out of order. My favourite example is paying off a
credit card every month, which is normally thought of as a
sensible policy, yet one which could not be followed by everyone,
since if it were the issuing banks would make no profit from
issuing credit cards and they would cease to exist.

Basic constants

Hume himself was not at all perturbed by threats of nihilism,
scepticism or relativism. He relied upon basic constants of human
nature, rather than reason, to keep us in line. He thought it was
natural to dislike the usual causes of distress, such as pain, ill-
health, misery, incapacity, lack of liberty or lack of respect. And it
was natural to admire characteristics which are 'useful or agreeable' to their owner or to others with whom he interacts: virtues
such as cheerfulness, sociability, politeness, intelligence, dexterity
and above all benevolence. These natural tendencies give rise to
forces that mould our characters into more or less acceptable
shapes. They show us who to dislike and who to admire, and in
the later work of Adam Smith, we 'internalize' the same voices,
becoming uncomfortable with our own conduct when we realize
we would have little or no defence against the criticism of others.
There is no guarantee that all human beings will converge on just
the same ethics, for our tastes and situations and necessities are
different. But there is a very good chance of convergence on the
essential core or heartland of good conduct, which is admiration
of the 'party of mankind', or those whose intelligence and benevolence makes them fit objects of gratitude.

  Does reason then have nothing to do with behaving well?

Having the right beliefs about the situation in which we act is of course essential to acting well, and here reason, in the sense of good empirical apprehension, is of course vital. Reason, in the sense of reflection, can also bring to light distinctions and subtleties, ways in which some conduct may deserve admiration whereas other conduct, superficially similar, may not. We cannot act well without reflection on our situation and the general principles we can feel justified in following.

It may seem from this brief account that practical reason and reasoning about what to believe are pretty much on all fours. But in practice this is far from being the case. In political and practical counsels, authority attaches to the reasonings of scientists and others about what is the case, whereas principles advocating what should be done about it receive much less respect. It is not only the rebellious adolescent who, when told that he should be polite or respect the property of others, is apt to reply with a contemptuous 'Who says?' Men of business and men of the world are little better. They often have a conservative and authoritarian face when telling others what to do, but quickly dissolve into scepticism when challenged about the propriety of what they themselves are doing. This is so even when the trespass is not so much moral as logical. A committee on public health and drug policy may feel little shame at accepting that (a) drug policy should be aimed at protecting people's health, (b) alcohol is much more harmful to people's health than cannabis and (c) it is appropriate that cannabis be illegal but alcohol not. This is in fact the status quo in the USA, Britain and many other countries. It is only philosophers, and of course those who suffer under the law, who weep about it.

How Can I Lie to Myself?
Self-deception, seduction and motivation

It is shocking to suppose I should ever stoop to such a thing as lying to myself. But others do, of course. The mother knows her child is a bit naughty, but stoutly and sincerely dismisses the very idea. The banker is utterly convinced that his gambles and loans will pay off, although he knows the failure rates. The partygoer knows he is unfit to drive, but stoutly and sincerely maintains that he is fine.

Too many of us too much of the time seem to live in a bubble of self-image that is falsely self-induced. Religious thinkers have always stressed the pervasive siren voices of self-deception and the need to be on our guard against them. 'Know thyself' was the motto on the oracle at Delphi, implying that it is quite hard to do so; the poet Robert Burns lamented that we cannot see ourselves as others see us. So if self-deception is so endemic, why is there any difficulty in the notion?

Both criminal and victim

The problem is that if the words are taken literally then it seems that the person who deceives himself or herself is at the same time both culprit and victim. If it is done intentionally, then the same person, as culprit, knows 'I am not fit to drive' and then plots something along these lines: 'If I believe that I am not fit to drive I shall be ashamed and upset and unhappy, so I had better not believe it: let me tell myself that it is not true.' Then, putting off his persona as culprit, the same person, putting on his hat as victim, receives the message that he is fit to drive, and gratefully accepts it. And this seems paradoxical: how can one person, at the same time, both know that he is not fit to drive and believe that he is? For deception to be a sensible project, it would seem necessary that the other person does not know the truth already. You cannot deceive me by whispering in my ear that I cannot read, because I know that I can. But with self-deception the agent knows something, but deceivingly tells himself something else, thereby getting himself to believe it after all.

Jean-Paul Sartre's famous discussion put the problem crisply:

I must as deceiver know the truth that is masked from me as the one deceived. Better yet, I must know that truth very precisely, in order to hide it from myself the more carefully – and this not at two different moments of temporality, which would permit us to re-establish a semblance of duality, but in the unitary structure of one and the same project.

The 'semblance of duality' Sartre thinks is lacking would be some way of modelling self-deception on the usual case of one person deceiving another. This might be true if we imagine the process taking time. The standard case is Blaise Pascal's. Pascal's celebrated wager says that you stand to gain a lot and to lose nothing important if you believe the central tenets of Roman

Catholicism. It is a can win, can't lose option. But it is difficult to believe those tenets, all the same. The solution is to put yourself through a process: go and associate with priests and old women, throw yourself into the whole thing, and you will end up believing. This is a drawn-out process of active self-deception. But there is nothing paradoxical about it because at no time do you both disbelieve, and believe, these doctrines. You transform yourself from someone who does one to someone who does the other, if the technique works. But the paradoxical case concerns what is true of an agent at one time.

Homunculi

Some writers have thought we should maintain Sartre's dualism by splitting up the mind into different subsystems, each with its own mini-psychology. So in the case of the driver after the party, perhaps there is one system, A, which is made anxious and unhappy by the thought that the person can't drive safely (let us call this thought BAD). And the other system, K, knows BAD but, protectively as it were, sets about making sure that A does not get to learn of it. The most prominent theory of this kind is the Freudian one, in which unconscious mechanisms of 'repression' keep unwelcome thoughts away from the conscious mind, banishing them to the unconscious. On this account, A would be the aware or conscious mind, innocent and gullible, and K is the unconscious, knowledgeable and deceptive bit. It is a matter of splitting the one person, me or you, into two 'homunculi' or little agents inside.

The problem with this is not with the very idea of unconscious thought. In one perfectly good sense a lot of what we think is

unconscious. I have thought for ages that camels do not naturally occur in Siberia, but until this moment, when it popped into
my head as an example, I doubt if I ever consciously entertained
the thought. The real problem is with what we have to suppose
about these homunculi or subsystems. Thus K not only knows
BAD but is motivated to protect A from believing it. K typically
does this by getting the subject to dismiss evidence for BAD (I
always lose my train of thought when I am tired; anyone could
trip up on a rug like that; I wasn't slurring but imitating Sean
Connery . . .). Or, it might manufacture countervailing thoughts
(white wine contains scarcely any alcohol; it has less effect when
you have eaten a meal; these are really small glasses). Or, it might
evasively turn my attention elsewhere (just look at that girl over
there). Or, it might obfuscate the issue (it's awful how they per-
secute motorists – it is all part of the nanny state; health and
safety gone mad). Yet all this happens without the subject ever
noticing the deception. In an influential paper Mark Johnston
pointedly asks how K manages all this: 'Do such deceiving subsystems have a much higher alcohol tolerance than their hosts?'

It is not plain either what motivates K to deceive A. It would
be good for the person, who owns both K and A, to face up to
BAD, even if he does not want to. So it cannot be as if K has the
whole person's interests at heart. If it did, it would take over
from A, the stupid and deceived other subagent, in directing its
owner to surrender the car keys. So what is K up to? And then,
why does A let it get away with it? As Johnston points out, if we
suppose that the deceived system A somehow colludes in the
deception, then the original paradox is reinstated, since A is now
playing a role in deceiving itself. And ethically, we do need a

degree to which an agent is responsible for his own deception. The self-deceiver who has convinced himself that BAD is not true after all, and who then weaves home and has an accident, is responsible for the idiocy of his behaviour. He cannot turn around and say that he did not know that he was too drunk to drive, that only some hidden subsystem K, which he is unlucky enough to have had foisted on him as an unknown part of his government team, knew it, but that as a result of K's machinations, he himself did not. After all, in interpersonal cases, if I genuinely do not know something, and am deceived by you into believing something untrue, it is you who are responsible for my error rather than me. I am the innocent victim. But self-deceivers are not so innocent.

The same problems beset the Freudian story in which there is a 'censor', a little agent or homunculus, who guards the gates of consciousness, making sure that undesirables are not allowed to enter. In all these stories the doings of we ourselves, the whole agent, are parcelled out to what turn out to be nothing less than whole agents within, with strange motivations and strange powers. But this does not do justice to the dramas of self-deception.

Being seduced

A better picture emerges if we recognize that it is nothing less than we ourselves who deploy the dismissive, countervailing, evasive or obfuscatory thoughts. We do this just because we do not want to admit BAD. We are motivated to these strategies by our anxiety or fear or dislike of what we are going to feel like if we do admit BAD to ourselves. The way to hold on to this aspect while avoiding the paradox is to recognize that we can mislead ourselves without doing so with the intention to deceive. What we have is a *motivated* strategy, but not an *intention* to deceive. This distinction is quite hard to grasp, so here is a way of thinking about it.

Consider for a moment some related mental phenomena. Many writers have noticed that people are quicker to believe agreeable truths than disagreeable ones. We raise fewer cavils if we enjoy what has been related to us. Indeed, David Hume diagnosed people's surprising willingness to accept stories of miracles, when they ought to know better, as partly a result of the 'agreeable passions' of surprise and wonder. Urban myths, and indeed gossip of all kinds, trade on people's defences being weak when a story comes along with the added incentive that it is pleasant to believe it. Conversely, we are quicker to dismiss stories which upset us, or engender the stressful business of rethinking what we were happy to believe before. These pleasures and pains provide motivations for believing things, but not reasons. They do nothing to affect the probability of truth. We do not intentionally plan to believe something we know not to be true; we just find ourselves believing things which, had our emotions not been involved, we would have had the good sense to doubt. We let ourselves be seduced.

Similar phenomena arise with rhetoric and eloquence, the use of language and gesture, intonation and expression of emotion. These all sway the imaginations, beliefs and desires of the audience. The devices of rhetoric are not appeals to reason but to emotion (which is why there has been a persistent philosophical tradition of mistrust of them). The orator generates a mood in which we trust him, or long to trust him, and at its most intense that mood can quite overcome our better judgement. Again, we let ourselves be seduced. In a somewhat similar way we might let ourselves be flattered, purring with pleasure, even although in a cooler moment we recognize that the flatterer was insincere, or trying to get something out of us.

As the case of belief in miracles shows, the desirability of something being true can swamp proper scepticism about whether it is true. The researcher irrationally convinced of his line of inquiry, or the partisan of some political position dismissing flaws in his case, are in the same boat. And there may be nothing to regret about this. Dedication to a cause may require the kind of commitment that rides pretty roughshod over doubts and self-doubts. Politicians who cannot summon up conviction are less successful than ones who can.

It is particularly painful to be confronted with our own flaws and failures. We all have to preserve our potentially fragile self-esteem. We overestimate how good we are at doing things, and there is evidence that the worse we are, the greater the overestimation. Things that threaten that self-esteem are particularly unpleasant. They provoke anxiety, and it would be much better if they were not true. So we have every motivation to prevent the truth from swimming into view. If the thought that a truth of this kind might be true so much as comes to mind, or if a pattern is forming which raises the suspicion, then we have every motivation to attack the messenger: to find ways of dismissing what is being suggested.

Motivation vs. intention

These are not yet full-fledged cases of self-deception. But they are quite close cousins; indeed, in some cases where the countervailing evidence is obvious enough, they blend into full self-deception. They do not involve intention. The deceived person enjoying the story, or pleased at the flattery, or swayed by the orator, does not formulate a deliberate plan: 'I must set about believing this, because I will enjoy it.' He finds himself believing it, and it is because it is enjoyable that he does so. His foolishness is motivated, but not intentional. When the teacher tells the pupil that his writing leaves a lot to be desired, and the pupil spends the next ten minutes vividly dwelling on what a curmudgeonly, out-of-touch, pedantic fool the teacher is, he is not intentionally trying to manipulate his own belief. He is just taking comfort in a mechanism that nicely diminishes the credibility of what the teacher is telling him. Again, his foolishness is motivated, but not intentional.

If we were wholly rational animals, perhaps the only mental state that could cause a belief would be the reception of a piece of evidence for it. Perhaps we approximate to this. Indeed, Donald Davidson thought we had to conform pretty well to this pattern or forfeit all meaning and intelligibility. If the causal processes whereby one mental state leads to another do not correspond to the one being a reason for the other, then eventually we are so totally at sea that the whole question of what we think or believe becomes indeterminate. We can get a feel for this argument if we imagine someone claiming, say, that their car is a live dog. If they accept that dogs have hair and paws and that their car does not have hair and paws, but continue to claim that it is a live dog, we have to throw up our hands. We do not know what they must be thinking. Once the wheels of reason skid this badly, the whole apparatus of meaning and cognition comes off the road.

While Davidson may be right in general, the phenomena of seduction and self-deception show that we are not wholly like that. Mental states can play a role in causing beliefs without in the least being reasons for them to be true. However, for our will and emotions to do their work, we may have to suppress contrary thoughts (this is the tribute that vice plays to the virtue of a purely Davidsonian agent). So the scenario becomes this. Suppose the situation is such that we *ought* to believe BAD. But BAD is threatening, and it would be better if it were not true. So we are motivated not to believe it. So we recruit the kinds of strategy already mentioned. We dismiss objections, dwell on countervailing thoughts, however flimsy, distract ourselves and evade our attention, obfuscate the issue with irrelevancies. We practise rhetoric on ourselves. We are not following a conscious plan of deceiving ourselves. Perhaps we would indignantly repudiate the suggestion. Imagine a solicitous spouse suggesting that we know we are unsafe to drive but refuse to admit it. 'Rubbish,' we say. 'If I were unsafe to drive I would be the first to admit it! I am just pointing out that I am not!' – thereby refusing to admit it. But we are actively misleading ourselves, all the same.

Do we know it all along?

If we deny, as I think we should, that we are intentionally deceiving ourselves, what remains of responsibility? How are we to blame for the process, if no wayward intentions are involved? Well, it is a mistaken dogma in moral thought that we are only to blame for things that lie full and clear within our own conscious thoughts. The familiar counterexamples include *negligence* and *perversity*. The negligent motorist may let his attention wander, and then be to blame for the result. The student with a perverse plan of study is responsible for his own failure. He should have known better. Here it is a lapse of knowledge that is to blame, as it often is in cases of negligence. The airline that fails to maintain its aircraft properly should have known about the hairline fractures, and is responsible for the ensuing crash. It did not intentionally bring about the crash, but it is to blame for all that.

These kinds of responsibility are exactly those on show when culpable self-deception takes place. The agent should have known that his boat was unseaworthy – the least inspection would have shown it – but it would have been an expensive and uncomfortable truth to confront, so he avoided it by allowing himself to be seduced by his own rhetoric: dismissing the evidence, dwelling on countervailing thoughts, obfuscating the issue; and thence, perhaps with forced jollity, putting to sea and drowning his companions. Of course he is responsible. It was he himself who brought about the catastrophe.

We may want to go further than saying that the agent *should* have known BAD. We may want to insist that he did 'at some level' know it. This is not reinstating the divided mind, or little homunculus K, the internal agent of deception. It is just that we have knowledge we suppress, prefer not to dwell upon, or allow ourselves to forget. There is only a porous and vague distinction between saying that someone should have known something, and that in this shadowy way they did know it, but refused to acknowledge it. They never avowed it to themselves. It has no voice. But we may have knowledge like that. We can discover, for instance, that we have known something all along: the little hints and traces, the glimpse here and half-heard conversation there, may not make us think to ourselves that our partner is up to something. But when the day of revelation comes, we suddenly discover, to our surprise perhaps, that we are *not* surprised, or as we say, that we must have known all along.

As their popularity in literature shows, the tangled phenomena of self-deception are very various, and endlessly fascinating. They undermine the image of the mind as wholly transparent to itself, as if we had a kind of panoramic view of our own mentality, and there was no corner so dark that we could not visit it at will. We do not need to partition the mind into a plurality of other little minds within to understand that we are not like that, and it is perhaps as well for us that we are not.

Is There Such a Thing as Society?
The individual and the group

The British Conservative Prime Minister Margaret Thatcher famously said that there was no such thing as society. She did so in order to praise the self-reliant individual, taking responsibility for his or her own actions, scorning help from the state, independent and self-made.

Society, or at any rate an ideal society, would simply be an agglomeration of these social atoms. And that means that there would be no interdependencies or bonds except at best any that might be freely undertaken, emerging from the individual self-interest of these atomistic agents.

Some social facts

So how much in the way of social bonding should emerge from our interactions with each other? Language, money and law, to take just three examples, are social entities, dependent on society for their existence and their function. Presumably Thatcher did not want to deny the existence of the English language, the pound sterling or the laws of the land (indeed the last two were something of a priority for her government). But if communication, money and law can emerge from the interactions of self-interested individuals, might not self-help societies, the welfare state or taxation of the rich in order to aid the poor similarly emerge? Yet these were the very things against which she wanted to stand, perhaps forgetting that however self-reliant we may like to be, at infancy and old age and many times in between we need each other.

It is tempting to imagine society as a rather mysterious kind of 'thing' emerging in some rather mysterious kind of way from what starts off as a mere crowd of individuals. Then it might seem to be no more than good, hard-headed, practical common sense to doubt whether there is such a thing. But that is misleading ourselves with the abstract noun. It is less mysterious if we consider the emergence of social relations from the interactions of individuals. Such relations have included those of communication, for which we need language; of transactions whereby goods and services are traded for goods and services, for which eventually we need money; and of guidelines for behaviour and sanctions for trespass, for which we need law. And then instead of simply a crowd of individuals, we have a set of structures, or in other words individuals bound to each other in complex webs of relationships. And that is what is meant by a society.

Not worth the paper it's written on

So how does it come about? With some difficulty, it seems, as we often see the process going into reverse, from examples of failed nation states and social breakdown. Evidently the structures are fragile and can collapse under us, even when they were once in place. This makes the task of understanding and sustaining them all the more important.

The classic analysis is due to Thomas Hobbes. Hobbes postulates a 'state of nature' in which individuals are not tied together by social bonds. Famously, he imagines it not as a Thatcherite paradise but as the 'war of all against all', and 'the life of man, nasty, solitary, brutish, and short'. How can people pull themselves out of this fearful state? Hobbes makes two unconvincing moves. First, he assumes that agents can get together and decide upon a common policy. And second, he thinks that their common policy could or should be one of submitting to a sovereign, or in other words voluntarily handing a monopoly of power to one agent, who, it is then assumed, will use the monopoly so granted for the benefit of all. John Locke's comment on this second stage is well-known, but good enough to deserve repeating:

> As if when men, quitting the state of Nature, entered into society, they agreed that all of them but one should be under the restraint of laws; but that he should still retain all the liberty of the state of Nature, increased with power, and made licentious by impunity. This is to think that men are so foolish that they take care to avoid what mischiefs may be done them by polecats or foxes, but are content, nay, think it safety, to be devoured by lions.

But philosophically the more interesting problems arise at the first stage. How are Hobbesian agents supposed to enter into an agreement? In fact Hobbes saw the problem clearly enough:

> *If a covenant be made ... in the condition of mere nature,*
> *(which is a condition of war of every man against every man,)*
> *upon any reasonable suspicion it is void ... for he that per-*
> *formeth first, has no assurance the other will perform after,*
> *because the bonds of words are too weak to bridle men's ambi-*
> *tion, avarice, anger, and other passions ... and therefore he*
> *which performeth first, does but betray himself to his enemy.*

It takes a precondition of minimal trust for me to enter an agreement to lay down my arms on your say-so that you will also do so, or to do a job for you on your say-so that you will return the favour later, and this trust does not exist in the state of nature.

If we postulate a state of nature like that of Hobbes, and a ruthlessly self-interested human animal, then perhaps the problem of getting more than minimal social relations up and running is insoluble. The minimal social relations that might exist would be those of reciprocity, where I temporarily sacrifice some of my own interests and do something for another, but only on the expectation that he will do something at least equivalent for me. Even reciprocity, however, needs assurance (I am just a patsy if I spend my morning getting fleas out of your hide unless I can expect you to return the favour), and in Hobbes's world there is no way to give that assurance. Someone once quipped that a verbal promise is not worth the paper it is written on. But in Hobbes's world, even written promises are not worth that either.

Evolving cooperation

We might reflect that Hobbes's problem is not, so far as we know, one that human beings ever had to face. There never was a state of nature, and we are not the egotistical monsters that Hobbes assumed (for more on human nature and on moral motivation, see *What Is Human Nature?* and *Why Be Good?* respectively). But from an evolutionary perspective, it might be felt that this just postpones the problem. The emergence of altruism is a problem if animals that sacrifice their own fitness for others must surely lose in the Darwinian struggle for reproductive success. So it is all very well saying that the human being is partly an altruistic animal, but if biological theory denies that any such animal can exist, we are still left with a problem.

The emergence of altruism is usually modelled by means of simple games, of which the best known is the famous 'prisoners' dilemma'. In such a situation it is socially best if we come to some cooperative arrangement. But each of us can look after our own interests best by defecting from this arrangement. In the original story, a prosecutor has two suspects, Adam and Eve, who are charged with a crime. But he needs a confession. So he gives each of them, independently, a choice to confess or not. If you confess, he says to each, then if the other confesses too you will be convicted, and serve two years each. But if the other does not confess you will get off scot free, for having helped the court. If you do not confess, he says to each, then if the other confesses you will be hammered as a hard case, and will serve three years. But if the other does not confess either, you will each serve one year on the lesser change of wasting police time. It is easy to verify that each of Adam and Eve has a decisive argument from self-interest for confessing: you do better by confessing *whatever the other does*. Yet if both follow this policy the social outcome is worst of all (four person-years in prison, when if both stayed silent they would have accumulated only two person-years in prison).

Many real life situations can be modelled as (multi-person) prisoners' dilemmas, in which self-interested reasoning will lead to a non-cooperative, worse, situation, yet the self-interested argument is good enough to tempt us. If there is a water shortage, the best social result is that we each restrain our usage. But if the others restrain their usage, my self-interest is better served by using as much water as I wish (one person's usage does not make much difference to the overall supply). If the others do not restrain their usage, my self-interest means that I had better not do so either: the water is going to run out anyhow, and I need to have watered my garden and taken my showers before it does so. Nice guys finish last, say the more ruthless beasts in the jungle. Cooperation is for losers. Greed is good. A landscape of trust and cooperation is always ready to be invaded by those who can exploit it for their own benefit, and these are the ones who will win out in the end.

Other social problems are better mirrored by a closely related structure, the so-called assurance game. The classic example of this is the stag hunt, described by Jean-Jacques Rousseau. We have to join together to hunt a stag: perhaps we each need to stop one of the exits from the wood, and if one is left unstopped the stag will escape. If we do catch a stag then we will each share the result, and that is best of all individually (unlike in the prisoners' dilemma, where confessing is individually better). Unfortunately each of us has a temptation to leave our post: there are hares about, and one can catch a hare all by oneself. Hares are good to eat: much better than nothing, even if not quite so good as a portion of stag. But now each of us needs assurance that nobody else will be tempted to chase a hare. If someone does, any of us who stand by our post ends up with nothing. Too great a risk, we might think, in which case we all chase hares, and end up with the second-best outcome all round. The sentiments voiced in the previous paragraph will quickly convince us that relying on other people is, once more, too dangerous. Winners know better.

Haystacks

So how could cooperation ever evolve? The question can be answered best by using an evolutionary dynamic. Imagine a population with a proportion of agents disposed to be cooperators, and others disposed to be defectors. Suppose cooperative agents' interactions are rewarded by them each producing two offspring of their own. But when cooperators interact with defectors, the cooperators produce none but the defectors produce three; when defectors interact with defectors, they each produce one child. This is the prisoners' dilemma arithmetic, only put in terms of benefits rather than penalties. If the cooperators are fenced in, then over generations they can begin to outnumber the defectors. The process can be shown if we imagine mice in haystacks for the winter. Suppose a population of C type mice and D type mice breed offspring of their own kind, and suppose that over the winter there is time for three generations. To begin with there are two mice in each haystack, with each combination in one. But at the end of the winter, there are sixteen cooperative mice, and only

eight defectors. The population will gradually tend to being one
of cooperators (see table).

CC	CD	DC	DD
2	2	2	2
4C	3D	3D	2D
8C	3D	3D	2D
16C	3D	3D	2D

Amongst human beings the haystacks phenomenon is not left
to chance. Defectors are identified and isolated. Only cooperators
are invited to play at the cooperative tables. Furthermore we have
signals – signs of trust and trustworthiness allowing ourselves to
be identified as willing to cooperate – and we have invented sanctions bearing heavily on anyone misusing such a signal by
promising to take part in a group enterprise and then failing to
do so. None of this is magic, and there are similar mechanisms
in the animal world. Amongst dogs the 'canid bow', when a dog
goes down on its shoulders, shows a willingness to play with
another dog. In some packs of dogs, such as the western coyote,
it sometimes occurs to a dog to gain an advantage by using the
signal, but then to seriously attack its off-guard playmate. Apparently if this behaviour is known to others in the pack, the
malefactor is subsequently more likely to be excluded and
shunned (a very serious penalty in animals that can only hunt
and exist in packs). In a well-running society, we are as good at
this as dogs are. If we were perfect at it, then defectors would
always be shown the door. As it is, in the peaceful parts of the
world, they get shown the door often enough to prevent their
invasion from taking us over.

Groups and beneficiaries

Darwin himself anticipated this kind of dynamic:

> *It must not be forgotten that although a high standard of morality gives but a slight or no advantage to each individual man and his children over the other men of the same tribe, yet an increase in the number of well-endowed men and advancement in the standard of morality will certainly give an immense advantage to one tribe over another. There can be no doubt that a tribe including many members who, from possessing in a high degree the spirit of patriotism, fidelity, obedience, courage and sympathy, were always ready to aid one another, and to sacrifice themselves for the common good, would be victorious over most other tribes, and this would be natural selection.*

Biology has generally been slow to accept this insight of Darwin's, labelling it as 'group selection' and somehow inconsistent either with the selection of the most thrusting and belligerent beasts in the Darwinian jungle, or with the insight that it is the survival of genes, in varying proportions, that drives the actual evolution of different kinds of animal. But there is no real inconsistency. Imagine a new method of treating an injury at football, such as a sprained ankle. Suppose it is quicker and less painful than the old method, which it then supplants. It makes little sense on the face of it to argue about which is the prime beneficiary of this change. Is it the ankle, the player, the team, the supporters or even the doctor? Is it perhaps the treat-

ment itself, a cultural device or 'meme' in Richard Dawkins's
sense, which will replicate itself effectively just because it is better
adapted to the football environment than the old treatment?

I do not think that these are very well-formed questions. All
that does seem clear is that there is an arrow of causation. The
change benefits the spectators because it benefits the team, which
it does only because it benefits the player, and it benefits the
player only because it benefits his ankle. You can't say it the other
way round: it is not true that the treatment benefits the ankle
because it benefits the team. But it could work from the group to
the individual. A change in the weather might benefit a player
because it benefits the spectators, meaning more of them come,
and there is more money for individuals in the team. It may even
benefit his ankle if he can afford better treatment as a result.
Similarly, an adaptive mutation in a gene may benefit individuals because it enables them to cooperate in a group, and may
spread because it does so.

In a very famous experiment Robert Axelrod asked a great
many game theorists to submit strategies for play in repeated
prisoners' dilemmas. A strategy might be 'Always cooperate'. But
it would stand to lose out if other strategies defect. The winner
of Axelrod's tournament was 'Tit for Tat': a strategy which started
by being cooperative, and then played whatever its opponent
played on the previous round. If its opponent defected, it would
meet defection from Tit for Tat in the next round. However, Tit
for Tat would then go back to being cooperative until it met
defection again. It was nice, but retributive, and yet forgiving –
a bit like some of us, in fact.

Tit for Tat can be beaten: it never wins more points than an opponent who plays defect, since it only plays one defection move in response. But when two Tit for Tat's play each other, or when Tit for Tat meets any other opponent who starts nicely and continues nicely in response to niceness, it garners three points per interaction rather than the one that is all defectors manage when they meet.

Margaret Thatcher's scepticism about society was part of a trend in economic and political thought. It was a trend that glorified markets as good and any kind of governmental inter-ference in them as bad. An economic market, the thinking went, is one populated by *Homo economicus*, economic man as the rational trustee of his own interests. Except in rather special cases of market failure, such as lack of competition or information, the market would then deliver rational and efficient results. In particular, the 'efficient market' hypothesis suggested that finan-cial markets, populated by information-sensitive, rational and competitive players, would always set prices that reflected a sum total of available knowledge. Nobody could trump the market. And government intervention in the market would always lead to a worse outcome than if it were left to itself.

As I write this, bitter experience is showing that markets are not streamlined, law-governed machines effortlessly pointing themselves at the best possible outcomes. They are more like the weather, or earthquakes, or turbulent flow in water pipes: chaotic, constantly at the mercy of unpredictables and populated by players whose sentiments and beliefs are highly various and highly susceptible to infection from others (what John Maynard Keynes called 'animal spirits'). Wherever the image of *Homo eco-nomicus* has been tested it fails woefully, because real-life agents are not single-minded, information consuming and economically rational. Many experiments, as well as common sense, tell us that they respond to hunches, dreams, fears and imaginings as much as to information, while in the last chapter we saw how self-deception is the human lot. They take misinformation in eagerly when it chimes with what they want to hear and reject information when it does not. They act out of loyalty, or desire for revenge, or a sense of fairness or injustice, as much as from forward-looking self-interest. It is delicious therefore to note that a theory built on *Homo economicus* in fact refutes itself: it is known that we are not like this, but classical economists, trained and rewarded in their careers for saying that we are, continue to say so, thereby exhibiting the falsity of their own hypothesis.

Mistakes in philosophy are not usually dangerous. But Mrs Thatcher's mistake was. If we believe that cooperative relations are mythical, that a landscape of trust will always fall to defectors who invade it, that values other than greed are just hot air, then of course we will live down to the ideology we have created. Belief in a spiral of decline can be self-fulfilling. Cynicism makes a world fit for itself, but the remedy here is better philosophy. As Keynes himself said:

> *The ideas of economists and political philosophers, both when they are right and when they are wrong, are more powerful than is commonly understood. Indeed, the world is ruled by little else. Practical men, who believe themselves to be quite exempt from any intellectual influence, are usually the slaves of some defunct economist. Madmen in authority, who hear voices in the air, are distilling their frenzy from some academic scribbler of a few years back.*

Can We Understand Each Other?
Treating words carefully

Obviously we can understand each other. If we could not, you would not be reading this, for a start. We understand each other at least largely because we share a language. Words have meanings, and when we communicate you pick up my meaning, and that is what understanding is.

Furthermore, our joint activities confirm mutual understanding in millions of unremarkable ways. If we arrange to meet at the university library at 11 o'clock, we each go there on the expectation of finding the other, and it often works. It wouldn't if you did not understand the joint arrangement.

Ideas and actions

So far so good. But mention of shared language only defers the problem. For what makes it true that you and I each understand the words and sentences of this language in the same way? What makes it true that we understand them at all? One suggestion is that words excite ideas. Their meanings are given by the ideas they excite, and we understand each other when the ideas in my mind correspond to the ideas in yours. This was in fact the suggestion made by John Locke at the end of the 17th century:

Words in their primary or immediate signification, stand for
nothing, but the ideas in the mind of him that uses them.

Locke says that with words men 'bring out their ideas and lay
them before the view of others'. Words enable us to give others a
kind of peep into a private cabinet to which the subject alone
has open access.

The issue of just what Locke meant by the term 'ideas' excites
a good deal of controversy. But he is clearly skating on very thin
ice. Suppose an 'idea' is a kind of private reproduction or representation of a scene. So perhaps I had a picture of the university
library in my mind's eye as we made our arrangement, and you
understood me because a corresponding picture arose in your
mind, stimulated by my words. The trouble now is that this
cannot be enough. We might share pictures, but unless we interpret the pictures as having something to do with the university
library, there is no reason for us to go there. The difficulty is quite
general, and does not depend on a particularly pictorial account
of 'ideas'. The problem is that this theory posits an intermediary,
a representative medium. But interpreting the representative
medium is itself an achievement of understanding.

The fact that you are looking at a portrait does not guarantee that you are thinking of the sitter, or that you even know
who the sitter was. To interpret a picture as a portrait at all is a
feat of understanding (or misunderstanding, if the painting
was not in fact a portrait). So the theory essentially involves a
regress: we understand words by associating them with items M
in our minds. And how do we understand items M? Eventually
there has to be a breakout: a change of focus from anything

in our mind's eye to the university library itself. For it is our coordinated action in going there that demonstrates our mutual understanding.

How to fetch a flower

This shows that the presence of an item in the mind is not sufficient for understanding. Ludwig Wittgenstein had a very beautiful brief argument to show that it is not necessary, either. He imagines someone being told to fetch a red flower from a meadow, and raises our problem: 'how is he to know what sort of flower to bring, as I have only given him a *word*?' He then imagines someone using the word to generate a mental picture of a red flower, and then looking for a flower that corresponds with it:

> But this is not the only way of searching and it isn't the usual way. We go, look about us, walk up to a flower and pick it, without comparing it to anything. To see that the process of obeying the order can be of this kind, consider the order 'imagine a red patch'. You are not tempted in this case to think that before obeying you must have imagined a red patch to serve you as a pattern for the red patch which you were ordered to imagine.

A wonderful knock-down argument. It applies against any theory which posits a medium: a third entity standing between the word and the library. We have to know that we have the right intermediary. And we have to know how to interpret the

intermediary, to use it to take us to the library. Each of these is
a feat just as mysterious as the ability we set out to explain. So
let us do away with the intermediary altogether.

What alternative is there? It is no good looking inside the
head, as we found in *Am I a Ghost in a Machine?* when we discussed consciousness. Suppose we found that when our agent is
told to pick a red flower, neuron X shows remarkable activity
(this is an extremely gross simplification of anything we are likely
to find, but will make the point). We might also discover that if
neuron X is neutralized and forced to remain inactive, the agent
is unable to obey the order. This might encourage us to think of
neuron X as the agent's representation of a red flower. But what,
apart from this role in underpinning the actions of the agent,
ties neuron X to red flowers? There is no magical projection that
associates this bit of grey matter with red flowers as a class (see
Can Machines Think?).

Instead we have to see the agent's meaning and understanding
as something that can be visible in his outer life. This means that
they can be manifest in his activities: the picking of the red
flower, in this case, or the journey to the university library in our
original case. The difference between people understanding the
words in a command, and people not doing so, is that the words
function as a guide for the first class, but just as a noise to the
second. Of course the guide is flexible: someone may understand
an order but not have much intention of carrying it out. But then
he knows what it is that he is not doing, and that in turn can
serve as an input, or guide, to yet further actions, such as eva-
sion or the manufacture of excuses. So the picture is of a word
triggering a pattern of activity, first in the brain, when it may

integrate with whatever else is there already – neural mechanisms underlying all kinds of other things laid down by the agent's previous experience – and then potentially in the agent's subsequent doings. This does not rule out silent, still, understanding. A person can absorb a message and do nothing. But it means that this is not what the system is for. Understanding is like the racing car's power: the engine may be idling or out of gear, but its power is shown when it is not.

Madeleine Bassett's problem

Now another threat to the sunny optimism that we do indeed understand each other opens up. My experience and its traces are different from yours. When you give me your words, the pattern of events in my brain is probably not much like the pattern in yours. If a third party gives us both an order, you may be minded to obey, while I am not, or you may burst into tears because of what the university library or red flowers remind you of, while I have no such problem. In countless ways the full, rather chaotic state of our neural mechanisms will diverge. So where, once more, can we find any sameness of understanding? If words guide us in arbitrarily different directions, how can we see them as the bearers of one stable meaning? If we always take words in our slightly different or dramatically different ways, why think of one meaning or shared understanding at all?

This line of thought can certainly issue in pessimism about stable and shared meanings. But I do not think that they should. If you burst into tears when someone talks of red flowers, and I do not, it may be that you are reminded, say, of your loved one's

funeral at which there were red flowers. But for you to think of
that, the words have already done their work. They have directed
your attention to red flowers. What happens subsequently is just
a consequence of that success, an optional add-on which cannot
affect the fact that you and I took the words in the same sense.

This may be the right thing to say in this simple case, where we
can indeed distinguish between the meaning and its associations.
What if the lines of thought are not merely associations, but
regarded by you as real implications of what has been said,
although not so by me? Here understanding can indeed begin to
become unhinged. Suppose like Madeleine Bassett you think that
stars are God's daisy chain, and that one is born every time a wee
fairy blows its nose. Then it becomes a little more unclear
whether you really understand me when I talk of them, or I really
understand you. We might appear to do so: if a third party says,
'Just look at the stars!' on a particularly fine night, we both look
in the same direction. And you must have a fair amount in
common with me for me to be able to say that it is the *stars* that
you are so completely wrong about, or that according to you it
is their *noses* that fairies blow. They are what you are attending
to, even if you have dotty views about them. Just as a shared
understanding was shown when we managed to meet at the university library, so it is at least suggested if we manage to look in
the same direction, and point out the same things.

Yet the second half of the 20th century was particularly a time
when philosophers became unsettled about shared meanings. They
gravitated towards the view that Madeleine's radically different
theory implied that what she meant was 'incommensur-able' with
what I meant, that we inhabit different thought-worlds, and any

appearance of communication between us was at best a fragile coincidence of behaviour which further experience would reveal to be accidental and unreliable. As a consequence, meaning became largely privatized. If I interpret you, it will be in my own terms. Seeing the world through my own lenses, I suppose that you must see it in the same way, and I interpret you accordingly. Whether we are writing the history of science, or studying literature, or doing anthropology, or translating or writing history, we will be reading our own meanings into things rather than original meanings out of them. We will be constructing meaning rather than finding it; moulding the words or other subjects into our own understandings. Interpretation becomes something like annexation or colonization, an imperial effort to trample over the conceptual schemes of others, dragging them into our own empires of thought.

Chaotic systems?

Not that those empires are themselves all that stable on this somewhat melodramatic picture. I may say what I mean now, but how will I take my words tomorrow? If I write them in a diary, there is no guarantee that my future self will take them the right way. He, by then, will have his own 'holistic' belief system. Just as his brain will have new connections and have lost others, so his thoughts will not be mine, but descendants more or less unfitted for interpreting me as I am today. In this bleak vision nothing is fixed; everything changes. And then even the idea that words, here, now, have real meanings starts to dissolve. If their meanings are not the same for one person at different times, or different persons at the same time, how can we talk of their real meaning at all? I may be motivated to say something, but what could possibly make it true that it means just one thing rather than another? It is interesting that this line of thought is effectively as old as Heraclitus, famous for denying that you can step into the same river twice, 'for new waters are ever flowing in upon you'. It was one of his followers, Cratylus, who, according to Aristotle, found the flux of things so disturbing to any notion of meaning that he was completely silenced, and reduced to communicating by wagging his finger.

Obviously we need to draw back from this abyss, and as usual the best defence against scepticism is to remind ourselves of homely cases. We can coordinate, communicate and behave intelligently in the light of things that we have been told and that we understand as they were intended. The mistake is not to recognize that stable and shared understanding is possible in spite of massive variation in underlying neural events or in other things and theories that we hold. In philosopher's jargon, the same thoughts can be 'variably realized' just as the same program can be variably executed in different computers, or in the one computer at different times. I have no idea whether the circuitry underlying my computer's execution of Word here at home is the same as that of last year's model in my office, and I do not need to know about it. When we agree to meet at the university library, it is enough if we execute this common project. I do not need to know what else may be in your mind, and still less how your seething brain manages to process the words. So long as the output is as it should be, all is well.

Humpty Dumpty and Davidson

We must also resist the view that privatizes meaning. The very first exercise of understanding is social, not private. It is in communication with others that language is first embodied in the developing mind. It is we, together, who determine and indeed who police meaning. An individual is up for being told what his words mean, if there is reason to believe that he has strayed away from them. Humpty Dumpty did not realize this, in one of the famous inversions that marked the looking-glass world:

> 'There's glory for you!'
> 'I don't know what you mean by "glory",' Alice said.
> Humpty Dumpty smiled contemptuously. 'Of course you don't – 'till I tell you. I meant "there's a nice knock-down argument for you!"'
> 'But "glory" doesn't mean "a nice knock-down argument",' Alice objected.
> 'When I use a word,' Humpty Dumpty said, in rather a scornful tone, 'it means just what I choose it to mean – neither more nor less.'
> 'The question is,' said Alice, 'whether you can make words mean so many different things.'
> 'The question is,' said Humpty Dumpty, 'which is to be master – that's all.'

Humpty Dumpty's mistake is to suppose that either words interpret themselves, which they clearly do not, or that he can make them mean what he wants. The truth is different again, namely that we, collectively, have made them mean what we want. The child learns its mother tongue by induction into a social practice, and it is by its so doing that its mind becomes a mirror of those around it.

As we touched upon previously (see *How Can I Lie to Myself?*), Donald Davidson attacked meaning scepticism even more radically. Davidson asked whether we can really make sense of the pessimist's talk of different people, or different groups, having different 'conceptual schemes'. He pointed out the vast amount that we have to share with persons in order to be able to interpret them at all. We can make sense of local conceptual divergence, like the occasional Italian word for which there is no English equivalent: 'simpatico', say. But in this kind of case we have workarounds. We can say, perhaps clumsily and at length, what the Italian means. Historians of science can tell us what people thought when they worked in terms of phlogiston or vital fluid. According to Davidson, we can only interpret others by seeing them as sharing our world, and sharing many of our own beliefs about it. That means, he argued, that there is a nasty dilemma confronting the notion of different conceptual schemes. Either we can get on all fours with the others, translating their words and understanding them accordingly. Or, if we cannot, we forfeit any possibility of seeing them as thinking at all. We lose any sense of mind at work, and are reduced to seeing only movements and behaviour, just as when words are mad enough they lose their significance and become babble.

Davidson's views about the methodology of translation and interpretation are highly illuminating and widely accepted. But the dilemma is unlikely to silence thoughts of incommunicable conceptual schemes. True, we may say, we cannot find ourselves in these others. We cannot hazard a guess even at what is going on in their minds. But it seems chauvinistic to make that all their fault, for having no minds for us to get inside. Mightn't it be partly our fault, or rather, our limitation? This is surely how we think faced, for instance, with the social world of dolphins or whales. These creatures evidently coordinate and communicate, but we share too little of their lives even to guess at the meanings in their signals. And it is not clear that we ever could, since their functioning is so far from our own (Wittgenstein said that if a lion could speak we could not understand it). We remain, and I think rightly so, in some wonderment whether this is just a necessary limitation to our chance of understanding them.

Fortunately, amongst our own species, we share enough common human nature for interpretation to work. We can find ourselves in others; indeed, it is how we discover ourselves as children. The Yorkshire saying has it that 'All the world is queer, except thee and me. And even thee's a little queer.' But not so much so that we cannot at least talk.

Can Machines Think?
Artificial intelligence and cognitive powers

It is tempting to say that machines must be able to think, since some of them do. We do, and we are just extremely complicated physical systems: machines, in other words.

But then we meet the contrary thought, that the fact that we are thinking beings shows that we are more than just extremely complicated physical systems, or machines. Because machines cannot think, but we can. Which way should we go?

The Turing test

The best approximations to thinking machines that we know of are of course computers. So we might explore the question by seeing what is at stake when we ask whether computers can think. They can certainly surprise us: chess-playing computers have beaten the most gifted grandmasters. Computers have proved mathematical theorems where mathematicians cannot (the best-known example being the famous four-colour theorem, showing that any map needs no more than four colours in order to avoid two areas of the same colour sharing a boundary, although the proof was in a sense 'mechanical': a matter of grinding through possible cases, very fast). We would certainly say that someone sitting in a chair working out the next figure in a decimal expansion of π was thinking, so why shouldn't we credit a computer doing the same with thinking as well? Computers monitor things, adjust things, warn us about things. So mustn't it just be prejudice, perhaps fuelled by mistakes about ourselves (see *Am I a Ghost in a Machine?*), to find it hard to accept that they could do these things intelligently or thoughtfully?

At the beginning of the computer age the English mathematician Alan Turing turned this kind of approach into a famous test, the Turing test. He imagined a computer and a human being alike put behind a screen, and an interrogator allowed to ask questions as he wished. If the interrogator could not, from their answers, distinguish which was which, then the computer should be credited with thinking. In the 1950s many computer scientists were confident that machines would soon be built that would pass the test. In spite of years of work on artificial intelligence (AI), we are now less sanguine. We have to restrict questions quite dramatically for even the most carefully programmed computers to pass even quite restricted tests. It is important to see why this is so.

We first need to think a little about how a digital computer works. Its programs take in inputs and provide outputs according to fixed rules. A machine may be able to process data presented in various ways: as patterns of pixels on its screen, or as sound waves through a microphone. To effect a computation it has to turn any data into strings of 0s and 1s, or rather into patterns of electrical excitation corresponding to those strings. The inputs and outputs of the computation are these strings.

Eventually an output may be transformed back into something of more use to us human beings: a sentence of English flashed on a screen or translated into sound waves through a speaker.

Now, since the computation has to proceed according to fixed rules, if we are to build an 'expert system', one capable of passing the Turing test, we have to fill its memory with 'representations' of things human beings know. We have to give it rules for accessing and transforming the data stored in its memory, in response to the input. The input is treated as a set of instructions, the data is accessed, and the output is a function of all this.

May I sit on your lap?

The first problem is the amount we actually do know. In a classic attack on the prospects for AI, Herbert Dreyfus took the example of a restaurant visit. Suppose we have carefully loaded quite a lot of data about restaurants into our computer's memory. It can answer questions like 'Does soup come before dessert?' or 'Do people sit before eating?' or 'What do waiters do?' There will still be an indefinite, huge, number of things we know that it does not. We probably forgot to tell it that when people sit they tend to keep their clothes on but take their hats off; that they do not sit on each other or with one foot in their ear; that when they eat, they eat through their mouths; that if a gunman or a rhinoceros or many other things come in, they will probably stop eating; and even if we wearily feed it such bits of information piece by piece, we are almost certain to miss out as many more.

Even if this problem can be surmounted, we still face problems of relevance and combination. A machine may answer well enough what waiters do (serve food). So far, so good. Waiters do serve food as a rule, but a computer which simply follows a rule to say that waiters serve food, when it is asked what they do, is going to be quite unable to mimic our own flexibilities and adjustments to circumstance. What do waiters do if a gunman comes in? If a parade goes by? Well, that depends. If the waiter is an ex-marine he might tackle the gunman, although if he is an ex-marine with a disability or who has turned pacifist, he is less likely to do so. If there are children in the restaurant he might encourage them to get up and watch the parade, unless they are horrible little brats in which case he may be less likely to do so. We face what philosophers call 'the holism of the mental': the indefinite number of ways in which things we know interact and adjust the right answer to any given question. Even if we have put an awful lot of facts into its memory, we still have to tell it how to deploy them: what is relevant to what, and in what ways. And those rules in turn are ones we know how to bend and integrate with yet further scenarios, quite indefinitely.

We might sum it up by saying that it takes common-sense to know how to absorb information and to adjust what to think and say in response to it. Intelligence needs flexibility. The computer, being rule governed, is poor at that. Its stereotyped responses will soon give it away, or so it appears.

Which kind of engine?

There is another problem on the horizon, perhaps more fundamental than the holism of the mental. This is the problem made vivid by John Searle's famous (or notorious) thought experiment of the Chinese room. In this you are to imagine yourself in a room with two windows. Through one window come pieces of paper with meaningless squiggles on them. With you in the room is an enormous library of instructions of what to do with any particular set of squiggles, ending up with you having a piece of paper with other squiggles which you pass out through the other window. Now, completely unsuspected by you, what is in fact happening is that you are passing the Turing test in Chinese! The incoming pieces of paper are questions written in Chinese, and the outgoing ones are answers also written in Chinese. However good the instructions, Searle argues, you still do not understand Chinese. The Chinese speakers outside the room might conclude that inside there must be someone reading Chinese and understanding their questions, but they would be utterly wrong. You are simply registering the shapes, just as the computer registers the sequences of 0s and 1s. But you understand nothing of what the shapes represent. Similarly, Searle concludes, the computer understands nothing by the binary strings it manipulates. The appearance of thought and intelligence is a sham.

Searle's thought experiment is extremely vivid, and we may initially be swayed by it. But it is wise to think a little further. Is it in danger of proving too much? Suppose we allow that you in the room, and the digital computer, are *syntactic* engines, only responding to the shapes or syntax of inputs. Searle's argument seems to show that however deft a syntactic engine may be at passing the Turing test, it will not be a *semantic* engine, where attributing a semantics to terms means understanding what they represent or mean. But we have to be very careful about arguing that no syntactic engine could be a semantic engine, or we may end up proving that we ourselves cannot represent things either. For Searle's argument, if sound, seems poised to attack the very idea of representing things to ourselves.

To see this, we should revisit some arguments (see *Am I a Ghost in a Machine?*). There we considered a neurophysiologist rummaging around in my brain as I daydream of the boulevards of Paris. Nothing he finds has any obvious connection with the boulevards. What he finds are neurons exciting other neurons. Suppose you asked the question, 'Are there shops along the Champs Elysées?' and that sets me into my reverie, before I answer, correctly, that there are. There is nothing from the time your question hit my ear until the time I issue sounds in response that has any intrinsic connection with Paris. There is just a system responding to the pattern of sound waves (squiggles), unleashing a blizzard of electrical signals, and eventually issuing as output another pattern of sound waves. It seems as though there is nothing but squiggles, squiggles all the way down, so we ourselves seem to be syntactic engines rather than semantic ones.

Looking in the wrong place?

However we saw that this is not the way to search for consciousness (see *Am I a Ghost in a Machine?*), so we have to confront the fact that it is not the way to look for representation and meaning either. Searle is right that you in the Chinese room do not understand Chinese. But that is like finding that neurons do not understand English. It is I myself, the whole system, that does that.

So the question now becomes: what turns us ourselves from being just syntactic engines into semantic ones? Searle himself inclined to the idea that it was just a halo of biological glory: we are made of the right stuff, and computers are not. But that will not do. It leaves us on all fours with John Locke and 'God's good pleasure' (see *Am I a Ghost in a Machine?*). It is not as if we see how the trick is pulled by substituting carbon, that we are made of, for the silicon or other materials in the computer.

Other philosophers have pointed out that representations have a dimension of correctness and incorrectness, right and wrong. We can represent things wrongly, inaccurately, inadequately. But again, it had better not just be 'God's good pleasure' to attach rightness and wrongness to arbitrary physical squiggles. We need to understand in virtue of what power a representation ever deserves calling right or wrong. The causal consequences of things are not right or wrong: they just are.

Nevertheless, any answer must start with causal co-variation. Systems represent things by co-varying with them. An animal system is evolved to adjust to an environment. It is things in the environment which are represented by the electrical squiggles, meaning that features of the environment (the presence of a smell or a sound, a scene with one or another thing saliently presented) dictate features of the signal, and the eventual output of feeding, fleeing, or doing anything else. For simple animals, the output may be stereotypically related to the input: sniffing the pheromone, the male moth makes a beeline for its source. Other animals are more complex, with a more complex range of responses. An animal may, as we put it, fix its attention on a predator or prey, attuning its behaviour closely to what the object of its gaze is doing: here we begin to talk of the animal representing to itself the movements of the object, for instance by anticipating them, just as a chess player may anticipate the move of an opponent. And here rightness and wrongness at least get a foothold. If the animal reacts to a glimpse as if it is prey, but alas it is a predator, things go wrong for it.

Evolution has managed to unshackle humans from the environment in ways that most animals, at least, cannot manage. We can rehearse strategies in our mind's eye. We can dwell on things in memory, or anticipate them in imagination. This is the 'intentionality' or directedness of the mind. When the squiggle manipulator in Searle's Chinese room sees the squiggles, it does nothing to direct his mind; but when English words pass before me on a page, or through my head, they do.

New directions

If this is all on the right track, then what we would need for intentionality in a machine is first of all an analogue of this directedness. We might get that in a robot like R2D2 in *Star Wars*, programmed to interact with an environment. Perhaps it is a domestic robot, and when it gets visual signals from a cup on the floor, it extends an arm to pick it up or fill it with tea. Once its repertoire becomes a little sophisticated, it will become natural to us to use the language of thinking: 'Look,' we might say, 'it thinks the cup needs refilling,' and so on. We adopt what Daniel Dennett called 'the intentional stance' towards it. This might be our best way of predicting its behaviour. Seeing a dirty room, we might think that we had better wait until tomorrow before letting R2D2 in, because it will clatter around being in the way, since it has so much to do. People playing computers at chess may actually say the same kind of thing: this program thinks it needs to keep its queen on the back rank as long as possible; that one prefers to attack with its knights rather than the bishops, and so forth.

Some philosophers of mind think that once we adopt the intentional stance then that ends the issue. By allowing the machine to be described in these terms, we settle the question of whether it is intelligent or whether it can think, and indeed of what it does think (that empty cups need refilling, for instance). This position, called 'interpretationism', in effect sees all mental facts as ones whose existence is just 'in the eye of the beholder': if an interpreter certifies a person or thing as thinking, then it is, and if nobody so certifies it, then it is not. If that is right, the only task for a machine is to behave in ways that we find it expedient to categorize in the language of thinking, and that settles the question. Unfortunately, I myself think there is something fishy about that. It seems to leave the question of our own thinking untouched. It is one thing to say that I, capable of thinking that a cup needs refilling, might find it useful to describe an appropriately behaving robot as doing the same. But it is surely a step further to say that this is all that there is to intelligence or thought. We might worry whether our own intelligence and thought is doing all the heavy lifting. It possesses original or basic intentionality, and although it may bestow honorary membership of the club to this that or the other system, nothing has really been explained.

One thing we might experiment with adding is motivation. Suppose a machine has circuitry that monitors its own states (cars already have that, of course). Suppose it is built so that it makes distress signs when things are not as they should be, just as animals do when they are not flourishing. And suppose we introduce avoidance or searching behaviour, so that when a distressed state is detected, the machine trots off to find oil, or new batteries, or whatever it needs. Evolution made us like this, but we would have to design it into our machine. Again, we would find ourselves talking about its wants and needs and strategies for filling them. It becomes an agent to be reckoned with (it might knock you over if you are standing in front of the batteries). Its single-minded quest for batteries now looks to effect a transition between syntax and semantics. It doesn't matter precisely what strings of 0s and 1s enable it to perform (and after all, we have never known and are still far from knowing the corresponding facts about ourselves). What matters is that there is a level of description, an interpreted level, which proceeds by explaining its behaviour in terms of its need for batteries and oil.

If we return to the problem of the restaurant and the enormous amount we know and the flexible ways we respond to it, we may begin to doubt whether the Turing test is entirely fair. Suppose our R2D2 is taking the Turing test alongside me. One thing I can do, that it cannot, is to predict what people are likely to do by using myself as a model. It is not that I have ever been explicitly told what people would do were a rhinoceros to come into the restaurant. But I can run the scenario in my own mind's eye and use myself as a kind of litmus paper. I can run an 'off-line simulation', as it is called. I would certainly stop eating! And this leads me to answer correctly that people would stop eating. R2D2 cannot use itself in this way, because its system does not mirror those of other people. But it now seems wholly unfair to set him this test: it is parallel to measuring people from foreign cultures on IQ tests on which the answers depend on familiarity with English cricket or American baseball. If my acquaintance with R2D2 is limited, I might well be at sea answering the equivalent question about it. If I have not been explicitly told about its reaction to rhinoceroses I shall be just as stymied. I would fail a Turing test conducted by a panel of R2D2s.

There is much more to be understood about all of this. In particular, when I said that we have managed to unshackle ourselves from the environment, this means that our thoughts are not confined to things with which we are currently causally interacting. But that means that there is 'something more' to intentionality, or the directedness of our minds, than causal co-variation. And that in turn might prompt the fear that we cannot really learn very much about our own thinking by exploring the workings of even the most sophisticated control systems, and even ones installed in useful robots. However we think about that, the task of philosophy is not to substitute magic or despair for the piece-by-piece exploration of what thinking is, and how it is brought about.

Why Be Good?
Annoying behaviour and annoying questions

There is an attitude that morality is only for losers; that you are a fool if you let it stand in your way; that other people will do you down if they can, so better to get your blow in first. In Plato's *Republic*, Socrates conducts a long campaign against this attitude.

If you can get away with it

Socrates dramatizes the problem in the myth of the Ring of Gyges, which is recounted to Socrates as a challenge by one of the other characters in the dialogue, Glaucon. In this myth a shepherd, Gyges, acquires a magic ring that renders its wearer invisible. Wearing it, he enters the royal palace, seduces the queen, kills the king and usurps the throne. This is an excellent outcome from Gyges' point of view – and who wouldn't do the same?

> *Suppose there were two such rings, then – one worn by our moral person, the other by the immoral person. There is no one, on this view, who is iron-willed enough to maintain his morality and find the strength of purpose to keep his hands off what doesn't belong to him, when he is able to take whatever*

*he wants from the market-stalls without fear of being discov-
ered, to enter houses and sleep with whomever he chooses, to
kill and to release from prison anyone he wants, and generally
to act like a God among men.*

In other words, separate morality from its consequences, and
you will see that everyone regards it as a nuisance, an annoying
brake on their freedom of action.

The psychological theory implied here is that we only submit
to the imperatives of ethics when we find it in our interest to do
so, or are too afraid to do otherwise. Society of course is quite
good at instilling this fear: as individuals we do not have rings of
Gyges, after all. In the humdrum business of day-to-day living,
honesty is doubtless the best policy. Cheats and liars get found
out, and suffer for it. Unfortunately, however, enough people are
tempted to think that they can get away with it to depart from
the primrose path of virtue. In some circumstances, some people
will think it is a risk worth taking. And less dramatic departures
from virtue are common enough to pass almost without comment. Men of business may find themselves in prison for fraud,
but not for greed, envy or pride.

Socrates and subsequent classical philosophers devoted a great
deal of effort to a noble attempt to square the circle, hoping to
show that in spite of Glaucon's story, virtuous living coincides
with happiness. Quite regardless of the sticks and carrots that
society holds over us, we only behave badly at the cost of something in our personal flourishing or wellbeing. The bad guys, on
this optimistic view, do not sleep soundly. They cannot contemplate their own doings with any kind of satisfaction or pride.

Like Shakespeare's Richard III or Macbeth, they are beset by
ghostly memories of crimes and sins. The lamentations of their
victims haunt their night hours. This is the revenge of the human
conscience on wrongdoing.

Flourishing

It would be nice to believe this, but unfortunately it is not often
true. Plenty of bad guys sleep perfectly well. They may even take
pride in their own ability to live by the law of dog eat dog (one
imagines Gyges having a good laugh about his ability to exploit
his luck). Or, they may be insensitive to their own failings, for
one of the sad facts of life is that bullies do not always see themselves as bullies; people who are pig-headed think of themselves
as simply reasonable; cruelty can disguise itself as kindness, and
so on across the spectrum of human weakness. Even the deliberate wrongdoer, who knows that he is succumbing to one or
another temptation, can bounce back with a happy grin if he gets
away with it.

If it is not always true that the wicked fail to flourish, neither
is it always true that the virtuous do flourish. This is the other
side of the classical doctrine, but no more plausible. Someone
may behave very well indeed, but torment themselves with the
belief that they could have done better. Very good people may
take on too much, blaming themselves for outcomes which were
not actually their fault. Or, they may behave impeccably, but
having suffered various misfortunes, regret not having taken
advantage of the occasional temptation that was offered, or that
other people seem to have fallen for without evident ill effect.

They might see themselves as victims of their own integrity, for instance. Following Socrates, the ancient school of Stoics elevated the coincidence between virtue and flourishing into the implausible doctrine that the good man cannot be harmed, the idea being that since his virtue is incorruptible, his flourishing must be immune to external shock and accident as well. This lofty ideal has its attractions, but a moment's realism suggests that the good man can indeed be harmed. The story of Job in the Bible is one of a good man being harmed, although it all comes right by magic in the end.

So if it is more or less a question of luck whether virtue coincides with happiness, why be virtuous? Some religions have a very quick answer: if you are, God will reward you in the afterlife, and if you are not, he will give you an especially nasty time there instead. If there is no justice here below, we can be sure it will all be put right somewhere else, or in another dimension of living after mortal death. It is a good story with which to terrify the children, but there is no reason to believe it. After all, if the creator of the universe cared that much about justice, why is the only example of his handiwork that we know about, the world as we find it, so indifferent to it? And in any event it does not give us what we wanted. We want to explore moral motivation, the concern for integrity or truth or honesty for their own sake. Attaching postmortem rewards and punishments to them only gives us another canvas on which we look after nothing but our own interests. Selfish behaviour is still just that, even when the gratifications it is after are supposed to come in a nebulous future.

One question or many?

It seems then that neither the classical tradition nor the Christian one provides us with much of an answer to the original question. To do better, we might start by querying the question (a typical philosophical manoeuvre). Why is the question being asked? Why is it more urgent, in people's minds, than the question 'Why be musical?' Or, 'Why like being healthy?' Or, 'Why help your children to grow up?' The presumption seems to be that there is something special, something more mysterious about moral motivation than other human motivations. But is that right?

David Hume explores this issue partly by reminding us of what we all know. We know, for instance, when someone is speaking well of us or speaking badly of us. If we are being called wise, careful, just, courageous, public-spirited, cooperative, dutiful and honest we might be permitted a small blush of pleasure, and might thank the speaker. If we are being called stupid, capricious, cowardly, selfish, uncooperative, feckless and dishonest we know we are being criticized, and are not at all likely to thank the speaker. We imbibed the evaluative direction of these terms with our native language. The same is true of many others:

> *Besides* discretion, caution, enterprise, industry, assiduity, frugality, economy, good-sense, prudence, discernment; *besides these endowments, I say, whose very names force an avowal of their merit, there are many others, to which the most determined scepticism cannot, for a moment, refuse the tribute of praise and approbation.* Temperance,

sobriety, patience, constancy, perseverance, forethought, considerateness, secrecy, order, insinuation, address, presence of mind, quickness of conception, facility of expression; *these, and a thousand more of the same kind, no man will ever deny to be excellencies and perfections.*

Since these features are admired, they are taught and practised, and if we are lucky enough to have a good upbringing, we will grow into them and then they come naturally. Being persevering, we keep trying; being patient, we wait for our delayed friend; being enterprising or discrete, industrious or frugal, we behave accordingly. We do not have to ask why: we just do it.

This suggests something more important, which is that there is no single question, 'Why be moral?' There is no question of the form, 'Why should I do what I should do?' – the first 'should' already gives you the verdict. It is not another piece of evidence in the case, but the conclusion drawn after the other facts about the case have been weighed. Of course, there are particular questions asked in particular circumstances by people subject to particular temptations. 'Why behave well here, now, in the face of this temptation and this chance of going unpunished by others?' is a question that can arise, but it takes a different form on each occasion. 'Why persevere, when I do not have to?' may be a good question, for someone with some particular task, but there will be no general recipe for answering it. It all depends on what the point of persevering, or the context, is. The answer might be: because you promised, or because it would let down the side if you do not, or because if you do you just might crack the problem, and so on and so on.

Looking after number one

Classical writers seem to have thought that any such answer, in whatever context, is incomplete or unsatisfying unless it bottoms out by referring to the agent's own self-interest. This is egoism: the idea that being reasonable in practical matters is entirely a matter of looking after your own interests. But that is a delusion. Consider the mother, asking why she should sit up at the end of a tiring day reading her child a story. The answer, 'Because it is something the child very much likes,' or 'Because the child needs it,' is a perfectly satisfactory terminus to the question why she should. Few mothers feel any need to go on and ask, 'And why should I bother about my child's wishes or needs?' and those that do excite us with a proper alarm.

Or consider the well-trained soldier or member of a college or club. 'Why should I do my bit?' might be a question that crosses their mind, but then the answer, 'Because it is what we do,' or 'It is expected of you,' or 'You would be letting us down if you do not,' is perfectly appropriate, and when things are going well, is perfectly final. It is just a myth that practical reasoning must finish with an agent applying a cost–benefit calculation entirely to his own self. We are social animals, and our concerns are, fortunately, more generous. We are perfectly capable of caring about others as well as ourselves, of substituting 'we' for 'I', whether the 'we' is a family, friends, club, tribe, country or humanity in general. Having been told that it would let us down if you did such-and-such, you have a thought too many if you go on to ask 'What is in it for me if I do not?'

It may of course be true that as we 'expand the circle' our concern becomes a bit blurry and sometimes a bit half-hearted. We may not love what does not touch us immediately with the same fervour as we love what does, and in spite of the moralistic injunction that we should, it may not be possible for human beings to spread their concerns so evenly, any more than it is possible to fear a remote event as much as we fear an imminent and immediate one. But the fact that we cannot spread our concerns entirely evenly does not mean that we cannot spread them at all.

Once the agent is properly socialized, he 'internalizes' the voice of others: the criticism he knows he would attract if he does something despicable, or the resentments felt by those he might trample upon. They become internal guides to which, willy-nilly, he finds himself listening. Few people, albeit too many, are deaf to these internal checks on conduct. Those that are deficient in social emotions are on the way to being psychopaths, rather than paragons of rationality.

So, someone's practical reasoning can finish with the discovery that doing something is bad for his family. It can also finish while pointing to the past rather than the future. 'Why should I be nice to X?' could get a perfectly satisfactory answer of the form, 'Because he did such-and-such for you.' Recognizing that an action is called for by gratitude, or a past promise, or a role that one has voluntarily assumed, is enough to determine a choice to pursue it. There is no calculation of future benefit, either to the self or to others. It is worth noting that animals are capable of this kind of motivation as well. In a famous experiment, primatologist Frans de Waal and colleagues discovered that a capuchin monkey given a lesser reward for performing a task, when he has just seen a fellow monkey get a greater reward for performing the same task, expresses rage at the unfair experimenter. He does not settle down happily with the lesser payoff (economists find this unintelligible, as do bankers and company directors in industry).

Here's looking at you

This is quite independent of the question of whether psychological traits that we admire, such as a capacity for gratitude, are themselves evolutionary adaptations, selected in the Stone Age mind because people with such traits leave more offspring than those without them. Such speculations may be true, but they explain the psychology rather than explaining it away (see *What Is Human Nature?*). Mother love may be an adaptation, but mothers do love their children. They do not love their genes.

All this is relatively sunny, but it by no means touches all of human life. The consequences of bad political actions do not necessarily rebound directly on those who perpetrate them. The law of the jungle is more apparent when it is a question of us against them than when it is a question of me against everyone else. Machiavelli noticed a long time ago that the prince, that is, the political ruler, must be prepared to behave much worse than the private citizen. Hence his notorious claim in chapter 18 of *The Prince*:

> *Therefore it is unnecessary for a prince to have all the good*
> *qualities I have enumerated, but it is very necessary to appear*
> *to have them. And I shall dare to say this also, that to have*

them and always to observe them is injurious, and that to
appear to have them is useful; to appear merciful, faithful,
humane, religious, upright, and to be so, but with a mind so
framed that should you require not to be so, you may be able
and know how to change to the opposite.

Politics is a dirty business, and it is quite possible that the good
political leader, as measured by his success in gaining or holding
onto power, or the relative success of his country as opposed to
others, had better not have too tender a conscience. This is so
even in democracies, or perhaps *especially* in democracies, where
the people against whom the crimes are committed, whether
inside the country or outside, are not the people whose votes
matter to the government. A politician may know that he is
breaking a treaty, or that he is lying about the aggressive intentions of a country on whom he has decided to declare war. He
may know that his victims know. But so long as the people who
vote do not know, or do not care, he may feel vindicated.

Perhaps we cannot find much of an argument to deter our
princes from following Machiavelli's advice, but then the path
of wisdom is not always a matter of finding arguments. In this
case the path of wisdom will include a free and independent
Press and other media, and a culture in which enough people
feel soiled by having leaders doing this kind of thing.

A course of experience can work on people's hearts even if
they are antecedently deaf to argument. One of the benefits of
trade and travel is that by bringing people into contact with one
another they work to break down barriers of insularity. Conversely, one of the features giving the infamous Massacre of

Glencoe its aura of particular horror is that the Campbells who set about murdering MacDonald men, women and children on the appointed night had lived with them for the preceding month. It was in Scots law a 'murder under trust' – more heinous than one which was not. And that seems correct. It seems that by commingling we do best to widen the circle of our humanity.

There are other reasons for thinking that forces of which we are barely conscious affect our actions more than arguments. A very nice result from a recent social sciences experiment is relevant here. In Newcastle University's psychology department there was a communal coffee provision, to which people were supposed to contribute a certain amount for the coffee and tea they took. Unfortunately, it seemed that people were not doing so. Like tax dodgers, they took the chance to freeload. So some members of the department put up new price lists each week. Prices were unchanged, but each week there was a small photo-copied picture at the top of the list, of either flowers, or of the eyes of real faces. The faces varied, but the eyes always looked directly at the observer. In weeks with eyes on the list, staff paid 2.76 times as much for their drinks as in weeks with flowers. The researchers say they were staggered by the size of the effect. It seems that even a small stimulus towards imagining that we are being watched is enough to deter us from carelessness or cheating. The people who paid up were not given any reason to suppose they were being watched. But the mere thought of it, conscious or unconscious, seems to have done the job. Perhaps this helps evolutionary accounts of why religions persist (see *Do We Need God?*).

I hope that three of our reflections help with the question, 'Why be good?' One is just stated; that often what is needed is not an argument, but experience. The second is that often the answer is given by our natures, as they have been formed in a culture of social animals. The third is that there is no single question. There are only a multitude of distinct questions, which might be asked by distinct people facing diverse decisions and temptations in different contexts. No one answer fits all, nor is any final answer needed.

Is it All Relative?
Problems of toleration, truth and confidence

In 2005, on the eve of his election to the throne of St Peter, Cardinal Ratzinger, soon to be Pope Benedict XVI, preached not against poverty or war or greed, but against something called relativism, meaning the kind of attitude that gets voiced when people say, 'It all depends how you look at it,' or 'Who's to say,' or 'If it works for you, that's fine,' or in the jargon of today's young, 'Whatever.' More precisely, relativism is the view that there is no such thing as the truth.

There is only your truth, my truth, their truth. Any attempt to privilege one of them is nothing but a power trip, and at its worst, something like imperialism or colonialism, implying patronizing and disrespecting others.

Papal anxiety

I am not sure the Pope chose his target wisely, because there is a special problem in preaching against relativism. This is that the relativist hears such preaching in his own way, and even papal authority is powerless to prevent him doing so. The Pope is in the business of claiming to be an authority, or indeed the authority: God's voice on earth. So of course he has to bang the drum for his own truth, objectivity, knowledge, rationality and certainty. I am revealing *the* truth, he says. But, says the relativist with a shrug, that's just *him*. That's him campaigning for his own, very particular brand of closed horizons. That is his view, and I have mine, and you have yours. That's all there is to it, in the end.

One can understand the Pope being nervous about this kind of attitude. It also presents a challenge that philosophers try to meet when they defend the conservative view that there are real standards, and that not only in science, but perhaps even in ethics and aesthetics, history and sociology, we can aspire to opinions that are objective and reasonable, and even true. The opponents to fear are not so much people who straightforwardly disagree with some judgement of ours in these areas. We speak the same language as them. We point out the features of whatever it is we are talking about. We think that these features ought to sway them, and they point out the ones that, they think, ought to sway us, and this goes on until one of us is swayed, or we agree to differ, or we go to war.

The relativist opponent that irritates us is rather someone who thinks of himself as above the fray altogether. He has achieved a kind of God's eye view of the debates that embroil lesser mortals. He sees the operations of humankind for what they are, the historical evolutions of animals trying to get by, the various readings of differently calibrated instruments, the clashes of wills. He sees ploys and manipulations and exercises of power. He sees persuasion and spin. But if any of the participants start talking of reason and truth, he sees only the same again, with added tinsel.

Philosophical judo

This cynical or disengaged character is not new. He is the principal opponent of Socrates in many of Plato's *Dialogues*, and it took all Plato's powers of reasoning to suppress these Gorgiases and Protagorases and Callicleses. Plato invented the classic argument against them, the so-called peritrope. This aims to show that relativists are in some kind of self-contradiction. The idea is first to get them to assert something. So, for example, the relativist might say: 'Truth has been unmasked as the rhetoric of those making a move in a power-game. So, all opinions are equally good or equally true.' The Platonist now seizes on the consequence: 'You say that all moral opinions are equally good. But then my opinion is that some are better than others. So that is true for me; and after all, your opinion is only at best true for you, for by your own principles you cannot advance it as true absolutely.'

This is a neat judo flip of an argument, and has been echoed by a great many eminent, and otherwise divergent, modern philosophers. A pointed application of it is a familiar problem with Marxism. Marx thinks that all values are ideology: that is, they are the result of particular economic forces at particular times, and have no further transhistorical authority. But he also *holds* various values, for instance that the world in which communism reigns will be intrinsically fairer and more just than the world under capitalism. There is a strain here. If this opinion is itself just a piece of ideology, as it appears it has to be, then how should Marx himself take it seriously? If he is aware that this is just the kind of view that you would expect from his class of the

intelligentsia at the particular socio-economic juncture represented by mid-19th-century capitalism, must this not dilute and
eventually destroy his enthusiasm for his cause? The problem is
that the relativist has to stand somewhere, while all the time
seeming to deny that there is anywhere to stand.

It looks as though this trouble will arise whenever the doctrine is applied to itself. Is the relativist then in conflict with
himself, needing both to advance the fateful claim – all opinions
are equally good – as really, absolutely, true, and yet to accept at
the same time that it is at best modestly true, true only for
him, now?

I don't think so. The relativist need not put forward his doctrine as more than the way he sees things. He can disclaim any
ambition to present it as 'absolutely' true. He opposes what he
sees as a particular high-flown and delusory conception of truth
in which some people clothe the stands they take. Such people
think you cannot have the activity of taking a stand without the
clothing, which is why they find the relativist suspect. The absolutist thinks that the dignities of truth and reason are necessary
clothing, robes of state without which our activities could not
take place, for they need these dignities. We must see ourselves as
lovers of Truth, and servants of the Good, so we must work to
make the robes of truth, absolute truth, fit us properly. Where
others see robes of state, the relativist sees only masks and disguises. But perhaps while belittling the robes of state, he can still
happily mingle with the carnival: making his claims, and even
hoping to persuade you of them, but not at all dressing them up
as anything they cannot, in his view, ever be. So a modest
relativist may escape the judo flip.

As usual in philosophy, when the sides line up so quickly, we might want to worry whether there is a shared mistake each is making. Here the obvious common factor is the view that truth and its handmaidens are indeed clothing, whether masks or robes. But suppose they are not? Less metaphorically, suppose there is nothing in the notion of truth, or even absolute truth, to be contested. Suppose truth is, as it were, too small to sustain the battle?

Letting the air out

Many contemporary philosophers of logic and truth think this way. They go by the name of deflationists. Suppose we think about truth for a moment. Suppose I believe something, say that cows go moo. I tell you, and you say, 'Yes, that's true.' You could instead have said, 'Yes, cows do go moo.' These mean exactly the same, and, say deflationists, that is the key to understanding *everything* about the notion of truth! If we think of any proposition *p* at all, saying or thinking or wondering or denying whether *it is true that p* is exactly the same thing as saying or thinking or wondering or denying whether *p*. It is as if truth is transparent, or invisible. Deflationists think that this is the key to understanding the whole concept.

Why does this make a difference to the debate? The idea is that the battle between the conservative and the relativist is sustained by a conviction that there are two issues, when in fact there is only one. For this battle to be joined, there must first be some ordinary issue. Since relativism often rears its head particularly noticeably when ethics is under discussion, let us take the ethical issue of whether capital punishment should be legally allowed. Then, participants in the debates about relativism think, there is secondly a philosophical or reflective (second-order) issue: whether there is a truth of the matter, that capital punishment should be allowed. The conservative says yes, at the cost of handing himself the rather cloudy vision of an ethical reality; the relativist will not pay this cost, and so says no. The deflationist, however, denies that there is any second-order issue. There is only the issue of whether capital punishment should be allowed, full stop. If we hammer this out, and decide that it should be, then we do not increase the theoretical temperature by adding, 'What's more, that's true.' This just repeats the conclusion that capital punishment should (or should not) be allowed, a conclusion to the moral issue with which we started. The allegedly distinct second-order issue gets swallowed up in the first, moral, issue.

Each side in the relativism debate got something right and something wrong. The absolutist or conservative was right that it takes some work to decide whether capital punishment should be allowed. It requires thinking hard about such matters as revenge, deterrence and the powers of the state, and these are confusing and contested concepts. It is not a judgement that ought to come tripping off the tongue. The relativist was right that anyone's verdict on such a matter will be a function of a good many factors in their background, including for example recent history, and other determinants of admiration, disgust, shame and pride. But neither of them was right that second-order reflection, focused on worries about truth, either precedes, or helps, or hinders a decision about whether capital punishment should be allowed. To come to an opinion about that, your gaze must be firmly fixed on capital punishment and the confused factors that suggest either that it is, or is not, a process to advocate. And once you have thought about such matters, you may be inclined to take a stand. You might then say, 'Capital punishment should not be allowed,' or, for it is the same thing, 'It is true that capital punishment should not be allowed.' Or, 'It is really true, a fact, that capital punishment should not be allowed.' Or, 'Capital punishment should not be allowed; you had better believe it.' Or, 'It corresponds to the eternal normative order that capital punishment should not be allowed.' None of these say any more than what you started with. We might have thought there was an ascending ladder here. But the ladder is lying on the ground, horizontal. It takes you nowhere.

Something more?

My guess is that the Pope would feel short-changed at this point. He thundered out the need for standards, real standards, and the philosopher has offered him only some very pallid version of what he wanted. He wanted to bask in truth, and hard fact. The philosopher says he has given it to him, but it wasn't much to give. Wherever you have an opinion, says the deflationist, you can express it, or you can express it with 'It is true that . . .' prefaced to it. It makes no odds.

Absolutists and conservatives who want more have tried to unseat deflationism. One argument is that we need to retain the idea of truth as a *norm* or ideal of inquiry. But the deflationist will reply that he can perfectly well retain whatever is valuable in that idea. It is a way, he says, of generalizing over a mass of claims of this form: you ought to believe that there is a cat in the garden if and only if there is a cat in the garden. You ought to believe that every even number is the sum of two primes if and only if every even number is the sum of two primes. Such claims can be stated without any use of a notion of truth, but we sum up the whole mass of them by saying that you ought to believe what is true. So deflationists say that truth is nothing but a 'device of generalization'. Similarly, the conservative may use what has become known as the 'no miracles' argument for truth, and particularly for truth in science. The argument goes that if science did not get us the truth, or something near to the truth, it would be a miracle that it is so successful. The deflationist says that what this amounts to is just that if you take a scientific claim, say that the electron has a charge of 1.602×10^{-19} Coulombs, then what is needed to explain the success of acting upon that is – wait for it – that the electron indeed has a charge of 1.602×10^{-19} Coulombs. Again there is no mention of truth anywhere. But this is science's own explanation of its own success, and there is none better.

If the conservative wanted anything else, this is probably something to diagnose and cure rather than to worry about. Probably, like Pope Benedict, he hankered after authority. He wanted an excuse from the heavy burden of judgement. He wanted the world to tell him what to think, in such unmistakable tones that everyone who listens is told the same thing. He wanted there to be a Book of the World, a voice in things, which we all have to obey. But there is no such voice, and could be no such voice. (Even the voice of God would be insufficient at this point, as Plato saw. For if God has not read the Book of the World, his voice will be arbitrary too: just another political pressure, as it were.) Young people become relativists when they realize that the voice of their parents and teachers is not the voice of the world.

This conservative hankering cannot be satisfied. But that is not a victory for the relativist. Remember the relativist's position is above the fray, taking the lordly, God's eye view of any debate. The relativist interjection, 'That's just your opinion,' is not a move even within a moral debate. It's a move to close the debate. But some debates cannot be closed, since over some things we cannot agree to differ. Agreeing to differ is often a way of denying that something is a moral issue after all, but perhaps a matter of taste or lifestyle. If you think capital punishment is a good thing, and I think it is never under any circumstances permissible, then we differ, and we may have to sort out our differences. It is not a matter of taste or lifestyle. If we try to sort the difference out, the relativist interjection of 'that's just your opinion' is spectacularly useless. Of course we are putting forward our opinions, since unless we are lying or insincere that is what it is to make an assertion. But we are putting them forward as opinions to be shared, or rejected. We are putting them into a public space, a space of discourse and reason. Their survival in that space is not a matter of their having a hotline to the Book of the World. Their survival is a matter of what to think: whether capital punishment is permissible, or capital punishment should not be allowed, or whatever the issue may be. The issue is the issue, not philosophical theory about the nature of the issue.

With deflationism firmly in mind, we can also see that there is nothing particularly imperialistic or colonialist about affirming some things to be true, and others not. Nobody could live a human kind of life without believing some things and disbelieving others that contradict them. And that is enough to license you to think that some things are true, and others not. It is not only hidebound colonialists who believe things.

Respect

If you think about it, it is curious that relativism presents itself as the philosophy that best respects 'difference', and that stands opposed to imperial and colonial attitudes to others. It sounds good to celebrate open horizons of thought, to admit that in the house of truth there are many rooms. But it is not particularly respectful to say that a tribe or a people or a person hit upon some truth, if you allow yourself to call true anything they happened to hit upon.

And relativism itself attracts suspicion and hostility for a good reason. Suppose I voice an honest and heartfelt opinion about anything, from mathematics to ethics to aesthetics. The conversation-stopping remark 'That's just your opinion' is not only beside the point, but more importantly dehumanizing. It signals that my words do not deserve to be taken seriously, but only taken as symptoms, like signs of a disease. Taking my words seriously would mean absorbing them into your own decision-making process, either finding them helpful or finding them to need rebuttal. They would become a factor in making up your own mind about whether, say, capital punishment is permissible or not. But if you look at me and see only the symptoms of a wishy-washy liberal ideology, or equally a harsh conservative vengeful one, then you are simply sidelining my words so far as the issue at hand goes. And that is disrespectful.

In the last decades of the last century there were virulent 'science wars' between honest-to-God working scientists, and allegedly debunking 'postmodernist' historians and sociologists of science. The scientist says, for instance, that the moon is about a quarter of a million miles from the earth. The historian or sociologist listens, but then goes into a story about how such a saying is the expression of an ideology or a perspective which itself arose for some identifiable sociological or historical reason: to assist the mercantile classes, or promote colonialism, or put down women, or whatever it may be. To the scientist this is insulting, since from his point of view the issue is how far away the moon is, and only then, and marginally, is he interested in the historical question of how people come to be convinced of it. His history of how it came to be believed starts with its being true: it is believed because that is how far away the moon is, and some very smart people were clever enough to cotton onto it, by finding ways of representing the distance in measurable terms.

Suppose I set out to explain why someone believes that there is cheese in the fridge. Two very different kinds of explanation might be needed. There is a boring one for people who believe there is cheese there when, and only when, there is either cheese or something that looks like it. This explanation goes along the lines of 'They looked and saw it.' There is a more oblique explanation for people who believe there is cheese there when there is none, and nothing that could easily be mistaken for cheese either. This may be more or less worrying depending on how explicable the mistake was: bad light, something that looked vaguely like cheese, or out-and-out hallucination. But any man with a white coat who resolutely sets aside the question of what is in the fridge, and then seeks to explain why I believe there is cheese there, is treating me as a patient or potential lunatic from the word go. This is why he is dehumanizing.

I have talked about a shared illusion, common both to conservatives and their arch-enemies, the relativists. Where does that leave us? It may seem as though the notion of truth is now very cheap, for after all, deflationism allows us to talk about truth everywhere: in ethics or even aesthetics, just as much as in science or mathematics. But although the notion is cheap, getting at the truth about many matters is certainly not. There are disciplines, such as mathematics or science, within which agreement emerges. Convergence of opinion is a more striking phenomenon here than in other cases. In disciplines of interpretation, such as sociology or history, and perhaps still more when questions of value dominate the stage, diversity of opinion seems more salient than convergence, and just as in classical times, this can engender pessimism and scepticism.

Science is convergent because it deals with things like atoms and proteins, whose natures are easier to know than those of immensely complex entities, such as human beings. Distinguished scientists, proud of the convergence that gives them what they rightly regard as knowledge, might look down on the divergent voices in economics, or social sciences, or humanities and the arts, and counsel that we stop doing serious history or political theory or ethics. That would not itself be a piece of distinguished science, but a piece of very bad advice. The science – let us say, nuclear physics or cosmology or molecular biology – does not give anyone a hotline into whether capital punishment should be allowed.

So we are left with what we might call the burden of judgement. Just as it took work and intelligence to determine a value for the charge on the electron, so it takes work and intelligence to think whether capital punishment should be allowed, or how to interpret a historical text or a piece of a constitution. I believe that this leaves a valuable understanding of where we have got to. In the heat of the science wars, any attempt to introduce a sociological or historical dimension into thinking about science, its emergence in the West, or the social and economic structures that underpin its activities, was apt to be met with a blanket accusation of relativism. But now that the charge dissolves, we should be able to see that in themselves such explanations are neither sceptical nor debunking, nor even disrespectful to the astonishing achievements and successes of science. Let us then close by keeping in mind two thoughts.

The electron indeed has the same charge in London or Paris, Delhi or Beijing.

It took a fortunate confluence of political, social, economic and cultural forces to enable us to find it out.

Those two remarks are perfectly consistent, and each has its own importance. The second should remind us of the fragility of knowledge, for it takes a not dissimilar confluence of political, social, economic and cultural forces to enable new generations even to understand the achievements of the past. Hence, it reminds us of the burden academics bear as we try not only to increase those achievements but even to protect what we have got.

Does Time Go By?
The strange river of time

It is standard to start any philosophical discussion of time by quoting St Augustine's celebrated puzzlement. 'What is time? If nobody asks me, I know; but if I desired to explain it to anyone who should ask me, then plainly I know not.'

We are creatures of time, living our lives in time. But attempts to grasp time itself seem to run into an impasse.

Time's turbulent flow

Perhaps we think of time flowing by. We talk of the river of time, of time passing, of times yet to come. The image is of the moving present. One moment in this year is present as I write this sentence. But it has no sooner come than it is gone, condemned to the grey shades of the past, and then to oblivion. Other moments await their turn, including the moment at which you, dear reader, come upon this very sentence in your turn. The special moment, the present, is moving inexorably onwards.

But if time flows, what rate does it flow at? Time seems to have no option but to go as it does: one second per second. Every hour takes just one hour, every day a day. But this is not a rate, any more than one inch per inch is a rate of growth, or one ounce per ounce a rate of putting on weight. To get a rate of change we need to think of a different magnitude that changes in time, such as distance from a given point if we are measuring speed, or pounds per week if we measuring our rate of weight gain. The rate at which a magnitude changes can itself change, as change becomes quicker or slower. The rate at which time flows cannot.

It is not only the rate at which time flows that is suspect. Which direction does it flow in? Perhaps we imagine the present creeping up on events which are still in the future. Or is it that time is flowing not forwards but backwards? Perhaps it is not the present that advances, but the river of time carries future and present events back, away into the past. Perhaps the present is immobile, and future events sweep back through it into the past. Any answer seems equally good, which suggests that we are in the domain of metaphors and images, rather than of literal truths.

We think of the present moment as singled out from all the others. It is the one that is special. We might even hold that it is the only one that really exists. The past has gone, the future is yet to be, so there is only the present. We might think of the present as something like the beam of a torch, with events illuminated only for a moment, and then returned to a darkness from which they briefly emerged. And perhaps in the darknesses of future and past, there is really nothing. This makes it seem enormously lucky, a kind of cosmic contingency, that wherever the torch beam lands, there is something. Yet we think of it as the most commonplace thing in the world.

Many philosophers, and perhaps the majority who have struggled hard to understand time, now incline to the view that because of these problems, it is best to avoid the metaphor of time's flow and the special nature of the present altogether. They suspect that the reality is what is called a 'block universe' in which there is no special present and no flow of time. This models time on the celluloid strip that makes a movie film. If we laid the strip out, there would be a lot of two-dimensional pictures in an order. Similarly, these theorists substitute a four-dimensional strip for a three-dimensional dynamic one. Each moment corresponds to a single frame on the celluloid strip. All events, past, present and future, exist like flies in amber, with greater or lesser distances between them.

The specialness of the present, such theorists say, is an artefact of our viewpoint, like the specialness of 'here'. All places are metaphysically on a par: 'here' has no particular privilege. There is nothing special about 'here', except that it is where I am, now. Similarly, they urge, there is nothing special about 'now' except that it is where I currently am on the temporal dimension. As beings living in time, we let the present fill up our foreground. But that is just like the view around here filling up our fore-ground, as it does. If we step back we can appreciate a different perspective, one in which 'now' is just one three-dimensional cube alongside all the others in the long train or worm of cubes that makes up the entire world in time.

There is a parallel here with other attempts to obtain a more objective view of the world than the one we normally have. It is often said that science aims at a more objective view than everyday observation and thought give us. It aims at a 'view from nowhere', free from the artefacts of human perspective. It dis-tinguishes objective nature from nature as it appears to us, with our peculiar sensory apparatus. So, for instance, while science tolerates wavelengths and energy levels of light, the colours we see because of them is 'down to us' – an appearance rather than a reality. Similarly, proponents of the block universe urge the merits of what Huw Price calls the 'view from nowhen', an atemporal perspective in which all of past, present and future lie spread on the one dimension of time itself. Change and becoming are relegated to a mere appearance that overcomes those living, as we do, within the temporal world. A more detached view abstracts away from them.

Imagining time away

Apart from these philosophical arguments, many philosophers and physicists have concluded that special relativity theory also casts doubt on the objective present. Einstein tells us that two spatially separated events can equally be seen as happening simultaneously or successively, depending on the way that the observer is moving in relation to them. But this means that the content of 'the present moment' is not itself a fixed, objective matter. The question of whether one event is past when the other is present has no one privileged answer. It all depends on the relative velocity of the observer. Of course, in everyday life we do not notice these effects, because we are familiar only with small distances, and small velocities compared with the speed of light. But if we travelled faster they would become apparent.

The block universe can seem incredible. Is it not substituting a static universe, a universe in which there is no time and no change, for the dynamic changing world that we know? The standard answer is that this objection also depends on mistaken imagery. When we think of the block universe as static, we are surreptitiously comparing it to things that in our experience stay changeless in time, perhaps like the granite tombs in the local church. They last ever so long without visibly changing. But the block universe does not have a mode of existence like that. It does not last for one time or another, because time is just a relationship between events within it. It contains the sum totality of all events in time. But its own existence is not an event in time. There is no measure that can be applied to it.

We might protest in a different way. Isn't time's passage just a datum, given to us as irresistibly as the fact that we live in a spatially extended world? In fact it might seem to be given to us even more inexorably, since we can at least imagine that the spatial world around us is an illusion, a long falsehood beamed into our heads by evil demons or mad scientists. But we cannot imagine time away so easily. Where there is consciousness, there is consciousness of time passing. Kant put this by saying that time is the form of 'inner sense' whereas space is the form of 'outer sense'. Time conditions events inside the head just as much as events outside it.

Even if attempts to occupy the view from nowhen meet a kind of failure, is it right to conclude that time's passage is a datum? Time appears to pass, but how would things appear if we indeed inhabited a block universe? Huw Price puts the reply especially clearly:

> After all, how would things seem if time didn't flow? If we suppose for the moment that there is an objective flow of time, we seem to be able to imagine a world which would be just

like ours except that it would be a four-dimensional block
universe rather than a three-dimensional dynamic one. It is
easy to see how to map events-at-times in the dynamic uni-
verse onto events-at-temporal-locations in the block universe.
Among other things, our individual mental states get mapped
over, moment by moment. But then surely our copies in the
block universe would have the same experiences that we do –
in which case they are not distinctive of a dynamic universe
after all. Things would seem this way, even if we were elements
of a block universe.

So we have to ask ourselves: what is actually given in our temporal consciousness? One thing is that we can affect the future,
but cannot undo the past. So there is asymmetry of some kind
built into the system, and the problem is to think through what
kind of asymmetry that is. We want that asymmetry, since
otherwise the image of the block universe might seem to render
all action and all care for the future pointless and futile. We get
the image of fatalism: that the future is already written, that
what will be will be, with all our efforts to avoid it doomed to
failure. God, we might say, taking the whole thing in at a glance,
looking at the busy ways we try to bring about this and avoid
that, must be looking down on us and laughing. In many myths
the gods foreordain an outcome, and it is made known to the
poor hero who then twists and turns and does everything to
avoid it, but lo and behold, it happens anyhow, perhaps because
of his very efforts. Is it really like this universally?

Inexorable fate

No, it is not. Fatalism should not be a consequence of our attempt to occupy the view from nowhen. Consider, first, ordinary causation in the world. This runs from past to future. If a brick drops into a pond, ripples spread out and a little later wash up on the shore. A view from nowhen sees both events and the temporal distance between them. But the view from nowhen does not see that the ripples might have washed up without the pond being earlier disturbed. It is not as though they 'just happen', or would have happened in any event. In fact, very likely the view from nowhen shows no ripples just happening, without previous disturbances. There is no perspective that shows that the ripples would have happened anyway, disturbance or not. Similarly there is no perspective that shows human actions have no consequences. If I throw the brick in the pond to amuse my children, they cannot say my efforts were futile because the ripples would have happened in any case. To make an omelette we must break eggs, and even the playful gods never see omelettes occurring on the timeline without eggs being broken quite close by.

Backwards causation?

If time's flow is unreal, then what is to prevent us thinking that current events may cause previous ones? Why not think that the later omelette caused the earlier eggs to be broken? Some have argued that the block universe view should loosen us up into thinking that perhaps this is a genuine possibility, unnerving though it seems. It might loosen us up to accept some of the more bizarre findings (or interpretations of the findings) of quantum mechanics. In the quantum world the state of a particle such as a photon can seem to depend not only on events *before* its emission, but on whether it is *about* to go through one process or another. Or, its state might seem to depend on how the state of a *different* particle is affected, although the distance between them is too great for a signal at the speed of light to affect it. It might reconcile us to these mind-blowing phenomena if we loosened up a little on the idea that causation can only work forwards in time, however fixed that idea may be in the familiar world. We might learn that it is only convenient or only conventional that we align the arrow of causation with the arrow of time, making it 'true by definition' that it is the earlier event that causes the later one, and never vice versa.

Perhaps we can get a feel for this by thinking of causation in terms of what philosophers call counterfactual hypotheticals – propositions like 'If he had not broken eggs there would not have been an omelette.' Breaking eggs was a necessary condition of there being an omelette. But from the block universe standpoint, might one not equally say that if there had not been an omelette he would not have broken the eggs? Causation itself is part of our perspective as agents situated in time. If we are to abstract from time itself, as block theorists ask us to do, then it is quite unclear why we should keep causation. There are just patterns. Some later events seem 'sufficient' for earlier ones, just as to us earlier events seem necessary for later ones. We, locked in time, have some trouble with counterfactuals that backtrack through time. We can use them, but we have to mark them as special: 'If there hadn't been ripples it would *have to have been* because nothing was dropped in the pond,' we say, rather than 'If there hadn't been ripples, nothing would have been dropped in the pond.' Yet, if someone with the view from nowhen examines frames on the film, he can use his knowledge of patterns to infer one way as well as the other. When a film is laid out on the studio floor, we can infer forwards or backwards. If we look at a few frames in the middle, we may be able to predict that there will be trouble, while if we look at the final frame and see that the hero and heroine have got together, we can infer that the villain did not kill one of them earlier. Inference works forwards or backwards.

This takes us again to the problem of describing the asymmetry between past and future, or the arrow of time. The problem is scientifically real, because a great many of the laws of physics are reversible in time. At a fundamental level it is normally true that if a process is physically possible, then so is its reverse. But, again, this is not how things appear. In the familiar world we see toothpaste coming out of the tube, never returning into it. Clouds of smoke disperse, but never coagulate out of surrounding air. Ripples never start at the edge of the pond and converge upon the middle, where they expel a brick. And we can remember the past and affect the future, but not vice versa. What, then, best explains time's arrow? The standard answer is that overall entropy or disorder is always increasing (the second law of thermodynamics). But is it a logically necessary truth, or just happenstance, that the order from past to future aligns with increasing entropy? We can certainly imagine the reverse: some have speculated that if the universe is like a yo-yo, and will one day cease expanding and start contracting, then there will be a systematic movement towards the highly ordered (and therefore highly improbable) state that must have come into existence at the time of the big bang. In this second phase of existence, ripples will spread inwards from the edge of ponds and when they reach the centre, a brick will pop out, toothpaste will miraculously coil itself back into the tube, and life will be lived backwards. We would all be in the position of the White Queen in *Alice Through the Looking-Glass*, who started yelling with pain shortly before pricking her finger.

Or would we? If the contraction phase is exactly symmetric with the expansion, then to me, say, living it, wouldn't it be just like living in the current increasingly disordered world? If we play Huw Price's thought experiment of mapping the individual experiences in this phase onto the four-dimensional block, then they will be just the same. If we call the times during this phase 't_b' for backwards, then my 2009_b memories will be of events in 2008_b while my plans will be focused on 2010_b! Perhaps it would be just like it is now. After all, from the standpoint of the view from nowhen, it makes no difference which way round the film on the cutting room floor faces. Then perhaps the difficulty of distinguishing which way around we are moving through time should reconcile us to the block view that there is no objective movement at all.

Back to the future

A final interesting question on which the view from nowhen may cast some light is that of whether time travel is possible. Numberless science fiction stories bring it to life, but none of them really convinces us that it could happen. The principal problem with thinking it through lies with what we might call the causal fertility of events. Suppose someone, call him Hero, steps into the time machine and finds himself in the world, say, five centuries ago. Now we have all learned that the slightest event may have the most extraordinary effects: the loss of the nail causes the loss of the horse, rider, battle and kingdom, thereby altering the course of the world, or the flap of the butterfly's wing causes or heads off the possible hurricane. Evidently Hero had better move carefully. He had better not rub out the events that led to his birth, at exactly the time and place of its occurrence, for instance. In fact, he had better not rub out anything. From the view from nowhen there is just one timeline, with particular events on it at each position. Perhaps this God's eye view shows Hero coming to existence at one time, t, and perhaps it shows him coming into existence at t minus 500. Either way, it is just the one world, and it never shows Hero's leap into the past.

Of course, from Hero's perspective, it might seem as though he is certainly in amongst the Italian Renaissance, or whatever. This is why film makers and science fiction writers can conjure up the scenarios they do. But from the standpoint of the view from nowhen, there is nothing to show. If Hero finds himself in an Italian Renaissance, it will not be the past Italian Renaissance, but at best one in a different possible world altogether, a facsimile Renaissance, in which he might throw his weight around as much as he likes, altering what would otherwise have been the case had he not barged in. But this would not be time travel.

I do not expect every train of thought in this chapter to convince a reader new to these difficult waters. But perhaps they enable us to join in looking at St Augustine with a new respect.

Why Do Things Keep on Keeping on?
Problems of constancy and chaos

Times change and we change in them. The world goes round, and things alter. But not too much. There has to be a speed limit, and fortunately there is. Our domestic cat will not suddenly start talking.

It won't even change into a dog overnight, and neither will I walk through a wall, or grow another pair of arms. In fact we think change only goes on in the comfortable shelter of things which do not change: laws of nature that determine the ongoing pattern of things.

Great expectations

Anyone reasonable expects things to keep on in much the same way. So what can reason tell us about these uniformities in nature? Here we meet an impasse. It seems we would have to give a reason for any constancy that we find, either by relying on empirical evidence, or by relying on something like mathematics and logic: either 'a posteriori', after experience, or 'a priori', in advance of experience. However, it seems as though all that our a posteriori knowledge could tell us is that at least if some things (gravity, strong or weak forces, some very finely tuned laws of nature) keep on in their old familiar way, then other dependent things will do so. If gravity continues in the way we know, then the solar system will continue its revolutions. If the strong and weak forces within the nucleus of atoms continue to work as they have done, matter will not fly apart, nor implode. But we can only argue for any one uniformity by relying on another one, until we come down to fundamental magnitudes determining such things as the strength of charge on the electron, the speed of light, or the strengths of electromagnetic forces. These seem to stay put, but why should they do so? Any a posteriori reason will simply push the problem back to some other constancy, onto which we then clutch. If we ask, in turn, why that keeps on keeping on, eventually we come to the point where there is no answer. It just seems to do so. It has done so wherever and whenever we have investigated, perhaps, so we extrapolate. We are confident that it is reliable, and will continue to be so. But is this any more than an article of faith, an unsupported dogma on which all our scientific constructions ultimately rest?

It is wrong to exaggerate this worry. It is not an encouragement actually to become nervous about our immediate futures. Our lives are premised on the supposition that the immediate future will indeed resemble the immediate past. Our best guide to what to eat is what we have successfully eaten in the past; our best guide to the number of limbs we will have when we wake up, or the language we will speak, or the place we will be, is how we were when we went to bed. We make structures of steel not iron because steel has always shown greater strength under tension; we expect to require oxygen and water in the immediate future just as we have always done. Anyone thinking these regularities are about to break in his favour (or to his harm, more likely) is deluded. Karl Popper was famous for asserting that all that science could give us are 'bold conjectures' as to what might happen (see *What Do We Know?*). But if the right attitude to a bold conjecture falls short of actually believing it, the comparison must be wrong. Our empirical science, our discoveries about the way the world works, give us more than mere hypotheses or mere conjectures. They give us our certainties, the beliefs which our whole lives presuppose. In fact, the philosophical sceptic arguing that we should not place any confidence in these continuities is wasting his breath. Nature forces us to expect things as we do. I cannot jump off a cliff without expecting to fall, or deliberately walk into a wall without expecting to be stopped, any more than a dog or a cat can. Our animal natures tell us how to navigate our world. They make us confident, and no reasoning could ever undermine that confidence. If, perhaps, some scientist got wind of a cataclysmic change on the way, it would be by relying on yet more uniformities whose relentless grip is about to destroy that of gravity, or the adhesion of matter, or the other forces which keep our lives in order. In that case, perhaps, we might not know what to think.

A straitjacket

On the face of it there is no a priori reason we can assign as to why radical change, chaos even, should not break out. What we would really like is a necessity, a straitjacket on events which (logically) *cannot* change. It would have to be something time-proof and self-sustaining, a law which, once written down, cannot be revoked. The ancient image of Atlas suppporting the world on his shoulders might give us a mythological glimmer of what we would like, but of course anything analogous to human fortitude is not going to be immune to time and change. Atlas, for all we can understand, might get bored or tired or distracted. He might shrug, and drop the whole shooting match. So to get what we want, we need a fact of a different kind altogether, and then the fear arises that we have no idea what such a thing could be: our understanding cannot comprehend it.

It would be much more comfortable if we could conceive of a straitjacket, something that is itself immune to the very possibility of change, and that in turn constrains nature to roll on as it always has done. In other words, we would like the laws of physics and chemistry and biology to be something like the laws of mathematics. Just as the law that between every pair of consecutive even numbers there lies an odd number is immutable, immune to time, necessarily true not just in the world as it happens to be but in any other possible world we can imagine, so we would like to find a constraining fact, a physical or metaphysical directive, ensuring the continuing good behaviour (from our point of view) of the natural order.

Unfortunately the best candidates physics can find for such a guarantor are simply more things that just keep on keeping on. These include the constant strengths of fundamental forces and magnitudes in nature. Cosmologist Martin Rees describes 'just six numbers', in his book of that title, on which the course of nature as we know it depends. They include the ratio of the strength of electrical forces that hold atoms together to the force of gravity (about 10^{36} to 1), the number defining the amount of energy released when hydrogen fuses to create helium (.007 of its mass), and other magnitudes each of which has to be just as it is, to within minute tolerances, if the orderly cosmos is to exist. Yet so far as we can see, such constants could in principle have been different, and could in principle change. Indeed, tests and measurements have been conducted on whether they *have* changed. For instance, it was speculated by distinguished physicists that the so-called 'fine-structure constant' which determines the strength of interactions between charged particles and electromagnetic fields has in fact changed its value a little over time (at present it stands at 1/137.03599958). Perhaps fortunately, in 2004 it was announced that so far as astrophysicists could tell, it has not changed. But there was never any suggestion that it simply could not have done so, like the structure of the numbers. Yet no amount of sophisticated astrophysical observations would help to determine that between any two consecutive even numbers there lies an odd number.

It is notable that if some measurement decided that such a constant had changed, the search would be on for something explaining the change. How would that proceed? It would have to find some other constancy which did not change. That is the way explanation works. So, for instance, it might be that the fine-structure constant has a value which depends in some lawlike way on something else, such as the amount of energy in the universe; then that in turn becomes a fixed point, an unchanging law, and the same old question arises: what on earth or in heaven assures that this relationship doesn't change? Faced with this treadmill, David Hume remarked that the utmost that natural science could do is to 'stave off our ignorance a little longer'.

Supernatural fine-tuning

Some distinguished scientists argue that the fine-tuning that these fundamental constants show is so vanishingly improbable, such an extraordinary set of coincidences underlying the good behaviour (*so far!*) of our world, that we must look to a divine explanation, both of the fortunate magnitudes they take and their fortunate stability. If the timeproof straitjacket cannot be found *within* nature, then perhaps it is best thought of as lying *outside* nature. This is a new version of very old arguments for the existence of a benevolent deity, guiding and sustaining the good behaviour of nature. A new Atlas in fact: a deity who is not only the first cause and architect of the whole show, but also its sustaining cause or ground, without whose firm control the whole cosmos might spiral into a void of timelessness and chaos.

The trouble is that our understanding is not helped by the instruction to look outside nature. A deity modelled on any analogy with human intelligence or human intentions might change, just as we do and just as Atlas might. So suppose the theologian rejects the analogy with earthly existence. Traditionally God is infinite, unchanging, beyond space and time, a necessary being that could not fail to exist and is dependent for existence on nothing outside itself. In a word, he (or she or it or they) is 'transcendent'. The trouble is that these adjectives sound very impressive but make it incomprehensible how he also interacts with the physical cosmos, either by making it come about, or by keeping it orderly. It becomes entirely beyond understanding, and while it is all very well to be told that whatever guarantees the order of nature lies outside the world of time and space, beyond our understanding, the downside is that if we cannot understand it then we haven't advanced our understanding by bringing it in either.

This puts an interesting twist on the old dispute between those who deny and those who assert the existence of a deity. The denier at this point is saying, 'We cannot understand or know anything about a transcendent reality that explains the ongoing order of nature,' while the believer is saying, 'We cannot understand or know anything about the transcendent reality, which is God, that explains the ongoing order of nature.' But since the inserted clause gives us no further understanding, the difference between them is best seen as merely verbal. 'A nothing,' as Ludwig Wittgenstein remarked, 'will serve just as well as a something about which nothing can be said.' Anything capable of sustaining the whole cosmos has to be beyond understanding, in which case it does not matter whether we say that it exists or that it does not.

Except, of course, that human beings cannot put up with this blank for very long, and begin to inscribe their own detail on the blank canvas in front of them. That is, they quickly go back to modelling God on a big chap in the sky, rather like ourselves, with eyes and ears and subject to human emotions and passions, such as jealousy or love or anger, or preference for our tribe against the others. But that part is no help with the cosmological problem. The more the deity is like ourselves, the more likely it ought to be that he gets bored, or tired, or drops the whole business.

Reason and faith

Returning to things keeping on keeping on, we might derive
some consolation from the thought that if our confidence is ever
betrayed, then at least we will have no knowledge of it. Our existence is entirely dependent on the delicate adjustments that keep
on keeping on. If they fail, then in a twinkling everything is over.
Perhaps we can accept the notion of time itself requiring the
ticking clocks of the cosmic order, so that if that order fails, time
itself comes to an end with it. In that case we could have the consolation that natural regularities will last forever, that is, there
will be no time at which they do not hold. But it is rather cold
comfort. We would hope that if the constancies last for ever, then
at least they will last beyond, say, next Wednesday. Being told that
they last for ever, until the end of time, but that unfortunately
next Wednesday will never arrive because time will cease to exist
on Tuesday, is not quite so jolly.

The problem we have been looking at is a philosopher's
problem. As already said, it does not affect our natural confidence in ongoing order as we conduct our daily lives. But in
some contexts, when emotions run high, the inevitable confidence in regularity can falter, and here Popper's description of us
as merely making bold conjectures can do real damage. Consider
that the standard timeline for cosmology and geology, the age of
the earth, the formation of rocks, and the evolution of animals,
is premised on regularities. The regularities include the rates of
a variety of kinds of radioactive decay, extrapolations from rates
of deposition and rates of formation of rocks and continents,
and other information derived from scientific analysis. These can

be coordinated and calibrated, and we can use them to determine that the earth is some four billion years old, and then give a timescale for the events in the geological record. But if we say that all of this is, nevertheless, merely bold conjecture we open the way for biblical fundamentalists and creationists to say that their 'bold conjecture' that the earth is in fact only six thousand years old is just as good a 'hypothesis' as that which science gives us. Careful philosophy of science thus seems to open the door to the most unscientific nonsense, and strips us of any rational weapons with which to counteract the nonsense.

What we need to say instead is that the creationist, just as much as the scientist, premises his life and his activities on regularities – only he then maintains the right to 'pick and mix' which ones he will choose and which he will not. His position is no better than that of someone saying that the world began five minutes ago, or that the creationist's holy book was written last week by extraterrestials from passing flying saucers, or that by flapping his hands he expects to fly. Once reason goes to sleep, there is no telling where we may end up.

This makes it wrong to say that our confident expectations are mere matters of faith. Using what nature is like and has been like in order to predict what she will be like is the only strategy which is not essentially arbitrary. It funnels opinion into confidence, and every day in every way such confidence quietly stands us in good stead.

Why is There Something and Not Nothing?
The strange ways of being

'Why is there something and not nothing?' is the fundamental question of metaphysics, and the royal road to religion and mysticism. It is uniquely baffling, yet it is uniquely difficult for people to turn their backs on it.

In his work, *Principles of Nature and of Grace Founded on Reason*, Gottfried Wilhelm Leibniz elegantly summed up the problem:

> [N]othing takes place without sufficient reason, that is to say that nothing happens without it being possible for one who has enough knowledge of things to give a reason sufficient to determine why it is thus and not otherwise. This principle having been laid down, the first question we are entitled to ask will be: why is there something rather than nothing? For 'nothing' is simpler and easier than 'something'. Further, supposing that things must exist, it must be possible to give a reason why they must exist just as they do and not otherwise.
>
> Now this sufficient reason of the existence of the universe cannot be found in the series of contingent things, that is to say, of bodies and of their representation in souls . . . Thus the

sufficient reason, which needs no further reason, must be out-
side this series of contingent things, and must lie in a
substance which is the cause of this series, or which is a
necessary being, bearing the reason of its existence within
itself; otherwise we should still not have a sufficient reason,
with which we could stop. And this final reason of things is
called God.

The drive for explanation

So according to Leibniz, there must be a reason why there is
something and not nothing, but this has to be a reason of a very
special kind, 'which needs no further reason' or which bears 'the
reason of its existence within itself'. Leibniz is here plugging into
a much older tradition in western philosophy, for from earliest
times the riddle of existence has driven humankind towards a
creator, a being lying outside the world whose doings brought
about the world as a whole. The being that bears the reason of its
existence within itself is quickly called God.

In a fascinating chapter of his masterpiece *The World as Will
and Representation*, Arthur Schopenhauer ruminates on man's
need for metaphysics:

> . . . *undoubtedly it is the knowledge of death, and therewith*
> *the consideration of the suffering and misery of life, that give*
> *the strongest impulse to philosophical reflection and meta-*
> *physical explanations of the world. If our life were without*
> *end and free from pain, it would possibly not occur to anyone*
> *to ask why the world exists, and why it does so in precisely this*

way, but everything would be taken purely as a matter of
course . . . temples and churches, pagodas and mosques, in all
countries and ages, in their splendour and spaciousness, testify
to man's need for metaphysics, a need strong and ineradicable.

'The balance wheel,' says Schopenhauer, 'which maintains in
motion the watch of metaphysics that never runs down, is the
clear knowledge that this world's nonexistence is just as possible
as its existence.' Advanced intellects, says Schopenhauer, thus
wrestle with the possibility of knowledge going beyond the
bounds of experience, hoping for knowledge of an order of
things transcending but explaining the physical and the empirical, while less strenuous intellects meet their need with the
'meagre fare' of the world's familiar religions, with their 'revelation, documents, miracles, prophecies, government protection,
the highest dignity and eminence . . . and more than all this, the
invaluable prerogative of being allowed to imprint their doctrines on the mind at the tender age of childhood'.

The void

It is noteworthy that as far as reason is concerned, there is no
direct association between life after death and the other doctrines
or imaginings of religion. The question of whether life after
death is even possible is a metaphysical question, and we suggested a negative answer (see *Am I a Ghost in a Machine?*).
However, if we think it is possible all the same, there is still no
particular reason to suppose it more or less probable if something like a personal deity exists and governs all things. In

principle, souls might be immortal (soul stuff is indestructible, perhaps) even if there were no deity governing the cosmos, and equally it might be that although there is a deity governing the cosmos, he (or she or it or they) may have decreed that souls only last as long as their allotted bodies, perhaps to avoid cluttering up his private heaven since if this is to be a paradise, it had better, not be overrun by riff-raff.

The problem with the religious answer was succinctly pointed out by David Hume. Our experience is entirely confined to things subject to space and time, things that come and go, dependent on happenstance and chance. Each of us ourselves, and each of the things with which we are familiar, is subject to creation and destruction, dependent upon the chain of cause and effect. This universal contingency of the things with which we have any normal transactions is admitted by Leibniz, and indeed forms his starting point. But Hume points out that because of this we have no conception at all of what something 'bearing the reason of its existence within itself' might be. We have no experience to draw upon. We cannot even get a glimmer of what the remote, inconceivable property of self-sufficiency could be. As a result, when we talk of such a 'thing' we are fishing in waters that are too deep for our little nets to trawl. Metaphysics thus stops in the face of a blank wall. (For what humanity does with this blank wall, see *Do We Need God?*)

If, nevertheless, we insist on following Leibniz's reasoning, the remote quality might just as well belong to the total cosmos as anything shadowy lying behind it. Perhaps because of this inconceivable quality of self-sufficiency, the cosmos just is. It required no external agency for it to exist; its existence is, as it

were, the default state. To put it another way, when Leibniz poses
the riddle of existence, he is presuming that 'nothing' is the natural state, the default state, compared with which the existence
of anything whatsoever requires explanation. But why should
that be accepted?

Simplicity and probability

One might try arguing that a state in which nothing exists is
somehow more natural, or simpler, or more probable than a state
in which something exists. Then there is a general presumption
that things which are unnatural, or complex, or improbable
require explanation in a way in which such simpler states do not.
In general this is a very dubious line of thought. First of all, simplicity often needs to be plucked out of chaos, and in that sense
it is simplicity itself that requires explanation. The exact distri-
bution of the molecules of different gases in the room in which
I am sitting is unique and unpredictable, and its exact description, if any micro-scale observer could give it, would require an
unimaginably long book. It would be much simpler if all the
oxygen molecules lined up regularly in one part, and all the other
gases fell into an orderly array behind them. But that state would
certainly require explanation, even if it would be much simpler
to describe. In physicists' jargon, it would be a state of low
entropy, an unnatural and amazing temporary oasis in the
encroaching desert of high entropy, random distributions to
which gases normally tend.

A second problem is that simplicity seems to shift with the
way things are presented. 'Nothing exists' sounds a simple

enough proposition, and one that for all we can see might have been true. But it is equivalent to '*This* doesn't exist and *this* doesn't exist and . . .' for all the individual things we can name, and then adding '. . . and nothing else does either.' And that looks like a very complex proposition, talking in turn of each of the vast aggregation of particular things that are denizens of the universe, and all the other things that might have existed but do not.

What about improbability? Is it more probable that there should have been nothing rather than something? Scientifically speaking, probabilities become fixed by frequencies of happenings. When heads turn up half the time in a sequence of coin tosses we home in on a probability of .5 for heads, or say that the coin is fair. Probabilities depend on numbers of happenings in empirically given, repeatable states of affairs. We can say that an event is improbable when we can find a repeatable family of events to which it belongs, but which deliver events like that one only a small proportion of the time. Snowfall in June is improbable in England, because statistics show how seldom it happens. But there are no statistics for first the state of there being nothing, and then the state of there being something.

We can try to imagine a real state of there being nothing (which is not the same as imagining a mere spatial vacuum, since physical vacuums buzz and shimmer with forces and fields). But there is no statistic to attach to the proportion of times this state of nothingness is succeeded by there being something. It is not as if we have a trillion cases of there being nothing, and in only one or two of them is there then something. We have no cases at all to go on. And if we do become convinced that the physical universe arose from nothing, then this was evidently a unique event, and as far as that goes its probability seems to have been quite high – it happened, after all.

And before?

Scientists now think that the whole physical cosmos came into being and was set on its course by a singular event, the 'big bang' some fourteen thousand million years ago. If we ask what there was before that, then the orthodox answer is that there was no 'before'. Time (or 'space-time') itself requires the succession of events in nature, the ticking of cosmic clocks, and before the big bang there were no cosmic clocks. The argument is that there could have been no measure of duration, no years or hours or minutes or milliseconds, so we can give no meaning to time elapsing. So we cannot ask what was 'already' there in the void, pre-existing the arrival of those things whose behaviour we know about. It would also seem meaningless to speculate about what 'caused' the big bang. Causation links events in time. Causes, we think, precede their effects, bringing them about. This is true of mental events just as much as it is of physical causation. Just as the earlier motion of a billiard ball causes the later motion of another that it hits, so a general's battle plan may cause the subsequent victory. But in this case too the plan must precede the victory. Hence there is no mental event nor physical event, nor anything that we can conceive of that is remotely analogous to them, that 'causes' the existence of the world, if space and time come into existence only with its arrival.

St Augustine already had this sophisticated view of time:

Then assuredly the world was made, not in time, but simul-
taneous with time. For that which is made in time is made
both after and before some time – after that which is past,
before that which is future. But none could then be past, for
there was no creature by whose movements its duration could
be measured. But simultaneously with time the world was
made.

The curious thing is that St Augustine happily goes on talking about the world and time being *made*. This may be sound religion, but it is on very thin ice philosophically. For *makings* happen in time, and presuppose a preceding state in which a maker exists and forms an intention that he then executes. To be fair, however, St Augustine notices the problem. He says that if we raise the question of what God was doing before he created the cosmos, an attractive answer might be the flippant one: 'Creating hell for people who ask questions that are too deep for them.'

Banging and crashing

If we cannot attach a scientific probability to there being something rather than nothing, we might nevertheless boggle at the improbabilities of the particular ways in which things fall out in the cosmos which we inhabit. The puzzle here is the 'fine-tuning' of some of the fundamental numbers of physics (see *Why Do Things Keep On Keeping On?*). We have no theory about why these things should have just the values that they do, but we can be sure that if they had been different by even a small amount, then things would have been entirely different. Matter could not exist as it does, nor complex chemistry, nor the stability of orbits of the planets around the sun, nor any of the circumstances on which life depends. So, as far as our scientific understanding goes, the precise fine-tuning seems to be almost miraculous – a conjunction of circumstances with an infinitesimally small chance of them occurring. But once more we have to be careful about probabilities. Once more we have no comparison class and no statistics. We cannot see a reason for these values being what they are, but we do not see a family of events in which they take some value, yet only infrequently take the values that they have. We only have the one event to go on, and since in that example the events turned out fortunately, perhaps it was probable after all, even if we can form no idea why.

Scientific regularities stop being guides to what must have happened in the first instants of the big bang, but it is thought that in a tiny fraction of a second the fundamental imprint was formed, so that subsequently stars and galaxies could form and the elements and the building blocks of life. If we continue to suppose that this must have been very improbable, we might try speculating that there exist a huge number of attempts at nature, a 'multiverse' with a huge number of big bangs, or perhaps trillions of 'little bangs' in which events never really got off the ground. Perhaps, indeed, failed bangs are going on at present, but fortunately for us none of them ever reach the inflationary stage when unimaginable quantities of energy and unimaginable temperatures come about and form the raw materials for a physical cosmos.

The speculation that there actually do exist a vast number of alternative universes, of which ours is but one, is just that – a speculation. It is not parallel to other pieces of science, in which observation and falsification can take place. In fact, the only reason for postulating a multiverse is to tame the supposed improbabilities. It provides a supposed number of events in which all possible outcomes do occur, so that it is no longer surprising that the singular outcome in which we find ourselves has occurred. But since, I have argued, the notion of probability is here being taken away from its home in repeatable sequences of events, the course of wisdom is to refuse it any application in these shadowy realms, and with it the notion of the multiverse can be retired as well.

Can we take any consolation by pointing out that if all these magnitudes had not had their fortunate values we would not have been here to speculate about why they do? If we knew in advance, as it were, of a multiverse of different kinds of cosmos, then it is only in the orderly ones that there can exist life forms capable of asking why they exist. So far as we know, it requires stability extending over huge tracts of geological time to give evolution the chance to develop complex life forms, such as us. Does this explain why our universe is orderly? Saying that it does is known as the anthropic principle or anthropic argument. I think it is wholly unsatisfying. The trouble is that within the world as we know it, anthropic reasoning is not a very respectable way of explaining improbable events that led to our survival. If some evil maniac makes me play Russian roulette a very large number of times, but I manage to escape without shooting myself, I might well marvel how it was that I managed it. But it would not be much of a reply that if I hadn't done so, I would not be around to ask any such question. The question how it was that I survived may well deserve an answer, even if I can only ask it when I did survive.

If the roads to an intelligible answer to the riddle of existence are as dismal and fruitless as we have seen, then perhaps Schopenhauer is right that it is only an emotional drive, such as fear of death, that causes us to go on hurling ourselves at the question. Otherwise, once we know we cannot get an answer we would surely be content with empirical science telling us how, insofar as it lies open to our gaze, the cosmos ticks. And it might help if to end with we touch briefly on the explanation of why the question is and must be permanently baffling (and therefore, arguably, permanently avoided or suppressed when it intrudes into our waking hours).

Let us waive the idea that time (space-time) comes into existence with the cosmos. Suppose instead that there was at some time absolutely nothing: no creator, no laws, no structure, no facts except the one fact: there exists nothing at all. Later on, we now imagine, there is something: let us say a big bang, or explosion of energy, plasma and the ingredients of the physical world together with a structure of forces of various strengths and perhaps other magnitudes. We, situated in the physical world, ask why it exists, and go into our normal explanatory routine. We look for a preceding event, causing it. But of course we know we cannot find one. There is only one characterization of the previous state: there exists nothing at all. So it follows that there exists nothing that can explain anything. We are baffled, but we deserve it, since by the very structure of the question we knew we would find no answer to it.

Of course, if there was already another 'something' – and here people will begin to imagine a God or gods with plans and

WHAT DO WE REALLY KNOW?

purposes – then perhaps the physical world is due to them implementing those plans and purposes. But that can only be a brief palliative. It is not answering the original question, for it simply turns attention to the question of why they exist and not nothing. And if we are happy replying that they just do, then we should be equally happy saying that the world just does. Leibniz was wrong. His principle of sufficient reason may generally give us good advice to follow: seek to understand the causes of things. But it is not anything more than that. In terms that Kant later introduced in exactly this connection, it is a 'regulative' principle and not a 'constitutive' one. It tells us in general to keep looking, and that is usually good advice. But it offers no guarantee that there is always something to be found.

What Fills Up Space?
The curious nature of things and their properties

At first sight the question, 'What fills up space?' is not one for philosophers, but one for physicists. Isn't it science that tells us the nature of the world around us? And the best science of stuff in space is surely physics. That is its subject matter, after all.

The reason why there is a philosophical component is that we can quickly start to puzzle ourselves when we consider spatial objects, of any kind at all, and then our knowledge of them. This chapter immerses us in the puzzle. Like Winston Churchill promising only blood, sweat and tears, I fear that on this subject philosophers can promise only headaches, and this is probably the hardest chapter in the book. It could be skipped, but there is gold in the mines.

Receiving information

Our knowledge of objects comes ultimately through sense experience. It is true, of course, that many of the things and all the most fundamental things about which physics talks are not immediately available to the senses, in the way that chairs and tables are. It takes sophisticated instruments to detect them, and sophisticated theories about the way the instruments respond to things to enable us to interpret what the instruments are telling us. But even when we know of objects indirectly, through instruments, it is our own sense experience that tells us what the instruments are reading. The same is true when we rely on the testimony of other people, who then serve as more or less reliable instruments for us to learn things. We have to hear or see what they say.

Whether we have to use instruments or whether we perceive objects more directly makes little difference to what follows. In either case we learn because the powers and potentials of things work upon us. We only know anything of things around us because we are ultimately *receptive*, or capable ourselves of being influenced by those things. In turn, that is because things have the potential to influence us. It is the power of the surface to reflect light that enables us to see it. It is the power of the object to resist penetration that gives us its impenetrability, or solidity, and the way we detect it by pushing into it. It is its power to affect sound waves that enable us to hear it, if it is noisy or if it deflects other noises.

Immanuel Kant thought this, and found it worrying. If we can only know objects because of their potential effects on others, their powers, then it seems that we are only responsive to what they *do* but not responsive, necessarily, to what they are. Kant thought that there have to be 'other intrinsic properties, without which the relational properties would not exist because there would be no subject in which they inhered'. But since the argument about our receptivity or responsiveness only to the powers of things is entirely general, it is not clear how we can know about this 'subject': it seems as if it has to exist, if Kant is right, but that we cannot actually know anything about it. And that seems shocking. Are we as cut off from the world as that? Bishop Berkeley, writing at the beginning of the 18th century, had worried in the same way that, if as was held on the prevailing views of his time, all we do is register the effects of things rather than their intrinsic nature, then really we are cut off from the world, caught in a 'false imaginary glare'.

Powers and dispositions

The argument also struck the great experimental physicist Michael Faraday, but Faraday thought that we could just do without Kant's 'other intrinsic properties'. Suppose we try to distinguish a particle *a* from the powers or forces *m* whereby it makes its influence known. Then, Faraday writes,

> to my mind . . . the a or nucleus vanishes, and the substance consists of the powers, or m, and indeed what notion can we form of the nucleus independent of its powers: what thought remains on which to hang the imagination of an a independent of the acknowledged forces? Why then assume the existence of that of which we are ignorant, which we cannot conceive, and for which there is no philosophical necessity?

The problem with this is whether we can be satisfied with the idea that 'the substance consists of the powers', or whether contrary to Faraday there is some kind of philosophical necessity to posit a substance as well, a nucleus or thing that actually possesses the powers.

It is important to realize that Kant and Faraday were not at all doubting the utterly familiar phenomenon of explaining the powers of things by citing other facts about their constitution or how they are put together. We explain the power of the clock to keep regular time by showing how it is made up from springs, cogs and mechanisms delivering constant impulses to the hands. That is fine, but the question is how to think of this process. If I pick out a cogwheel, say, then what I have in my hand is something I can detect. How? By sight (reflected light) and touch (it is impenetrable, and feels hard). Its powers act upon me so that I have no hesitation in delivering these verdicts. As I move it around, successive regions of space radiate the same effects: they in turn affect me in the ways that then make me judge the position of the cogwheel. In all this I am simply experiencing effects the thing is able to work in me and relating these back to the powers that it has.

But there is an argument that we need Kant's further category of intrinsic properties. We might call it the not-just-washing argument, after Bertrand Russell, who talks in his book *The Analysis of Matter* of how 'there are many possible ways of turning things hitherto regarded as "real" into mere laws concerning the other things,' and remarks, 'Obviously there must be a limit to this process, or else all the things in the world will merely be each other's washing.' The conclusion is that even if we have trouble understanding things apart from their powers, nevertheless we seem to need them. We seem to need them because otherwise we have no conception at all of the actual world.

If . . . then

Perhaps a vivid way of seeing Russell's problem is to think further about the logic of 'powers'. Powers are shown or manifested in actual doings if or when a test occasion is to hand. They are found when 'conditionals', or in other words claims about what happens *if* something else happens, are tested. Someone shows their strength when *if* they try to lift a heavy weight, they succeed. A glass is fragile when *if* it is dropped, it breaks. A space is occupied when *if* we try to occupy it, we meet resistance. A field of force occupies a space when *if* a test particle is put at various places, various forces act upon it, as shown, for example, by the way it then accelerates and the direction in which it does so. This is all well enough. Now suppose the events whereby these powers are manifested are in turn dissolved into changes in other powers. The test particle, for instance, is now thought of as no more than a set of powers, meaning that various further conditionals are true: *if* you direct your eyes or an instrument appropriately, there is some effect – an effect which again is deferred into yet another conditional. It seems that we are faced with an infinite regress of 'if . . . then . . .' claims, and are never able to reach a terminus in what actually *is* the case.

Consider the conditional, 'If you put your finger in the electrical outlet, you will get a shock.' We test this by imagining a scenario, or what philosophers call a possibility or possible world, in which you do put your finger in the outlet. If in this scenario you get a shock, then the conditional is acceptable. So 'if . . . then . . .' propositions are true because of what is true in imagined scenarios. Now suppose that everything true of our actual world is dissolved into a statement about powers. And suppose that powers correspond to the truth of 'if . . . then . . .' propositions. And what makes an 'if . . . then . . .' proposition true of a world is a question of what is true in imagined scenarios. Then it seems that truth is endlessly deferred. What is true is a matter of what is true in imagined scenarios, which in turn is a matter of what is true in imagined scenarios, which . . . As Russell said, we have to find a limit to this process, or we get the result that nothing is true anywhere!

Grounds

So perhaps Faraday was wrong, and Kant was right. We need the particle, a substance, or in philosopher's jargon a 'categorical basis' for powers, as well as powers themselves. We think that there are *grounds* to dispositions. Imagine empty space, but with two regions that differ only in their powers. If you visit one you meet resistance, experience electric shocks or meet other effects. Wouldn't we have to think of there being something there, an intrinsic difference in the two regions or in the neighbourhoods in which they exist, to explain this difference? It seems incredible that they might be identical, so long as nothing goes near them, but then systematically produce different results if something does. There has to be something *abiding*, something there, in virtue of which they have these different powers. Or so we suppose. But then, what idea of this 'thing' or 'nucleus' can we have?

Some philosophers think that categorical properties just *are* dispositional properties. This would be like responding to Faraday by suggesting that the missing nucleus or particle should be thought of as itself just the field of force, or in other words the sum total of the 'if . . . thens' to which it gives rise. But a cost of this kind of theory is that we can no longer think in terms of the categorical properties as *grounding* dispositions and powers. For they are themselves no more than dispositions and powers! Surely it takes something new, something different, to ground anything. In positing the particle we were hoping to posit something whose nature and position explained the field of force. If we cannot have that, we lurch back to the not-just-washing problem.

Russell was right. This is not a very satisfactory, complete, conception of a natural world. To put it bluntly, we can't be happy with an ontology only of potentials or powers. In such an ontology, a thing is no more than a locus of powers, or to put it slightly more accurately, a region of space with a thing in it is distinguished by its potential from a region of space without, and that is all. But what are these powers able to do? – Affect other objects, by deflecting their paths or giving them a charge or heating or cooling them. But these events, too, are just changes in the potential to change the potential of yet other regions of space. The realization or manifestation of a potential is just a change in other potentials. Truth is exhausted by what is true of potentials, coming and going. It seems that the whole physical universe has been spirited away into a kind of gigantic shimmer, nothing but potential, all the way down.

Getting us into the picture

One option, but a bit of a counsel of despair, is that we get away from the merely potential to the purely categorical, when *we* get into the picture. The effects of one thing on another thing, we might concede, are purely a matter of changing powers associated with different volumes of space. But when we become the recipient on which a physical power exerts itself, the effect is not just a change in our potentials. It is a change in our experience, a categorical or intrinsic change in looks or feels. So suppose a surface reflects red light more than anything else in a scene, and therefore looks red. The experience of red that I get when I look at it is surely as categorical as can be imagined. It is a felt change in my inner landscape. It is not like feeling a change in potential, as one might on starting to feel enthusiastic or energetic as opposed to listless and feeble. It is a change more in how things *are* with me, rather than how they are going to be if something else happens.

Perhaps it is right that it is reflection on our own experience that gives us our sense of what is categorical or intrinsic, as opposed to what is merely potential and awaiting realization by other events which are themselves mere changes in potential. But our own experience is singularly ill adapted to serve as a 'ground' for potentials. We are still going to be left with the two different regions of space, differing only in potential, even if we think that were we to come on the scene those potentials would get an ultimate realization in whatever flashes or bangs, colours, tastes, sounds or smells we would experience.

But perhaps that is all right after all. Perhaps Faraday beats Kant and Russell, reconciling us at least to a physical world that is nothing but differently powered volumes of space or space-time. Nothing really happens until we come on the scene and we have something like what is called in quantum theory the

'collapse of the wave packet', the sudden emergence of a real categorical event, an experience in us, out of what was hitherto only
a vast array of possibilities or probabilities or potentials for
events. (But can we imagine a cosmos made up only of an array
of potentials or possibilities or probabilities?)

When Isaac Newton formulated his laws of universal gravita-
tion in *Principia Mathematica* in 1687, the learned world was of
course electrified, but also disappointed. Fellow scientists com-
plained that while Newton had showed them what gravity *did*, he
had not showed them what it actually *was*. Newton shared the
ideal that something else was needed, but defended what he did
as the best description of the phenomena of forces, movements
and accelerations, which of course it was. About the idea that
there was something further to discover he actually said this:

> *That gravity should be innate, inherent and essential to*
> *matter, so that one body may act upon another at a distance*
> *through a vacuum, without the mediation of anything else,*
> *by and through which their action and force may be conveyed*
> *from one to another, is to me so great an absurdity that I*
> *believe no man who has in philosophical matters a compe-*
> *tent faculty of thinking, can ever fall into it.*

Newton here shows his distaste for a purely ungrounded, merely
empirical relation between what is true over here, and what is
true over there. If when there is a mass over here, there is an
accelerated movement over there, then he thought there 'has to
be' something mediating the production of the effect. It would
not be enough to say that this region of space has the power or

potential or probability of being followed by change in that other region of space. But the reflections of this chapter suggest that we may have to put up with exactly that: nothing but powers, all the way down.

I promised blood, sweat and tears, and I am sorry if at this point you feel that they were delivered. But now we lighten up a little.

What is Beauty?
The fatal attraction of things

Beautiful things can take our breath away. They can enrapture us, enchant us, perhaps give us a sense of wonder or awe. The experience 'takes us out of ourselves', a kind of ecstasy.

It can be fortifying and life-affirming, leaving us with a kind of glow, a feeling that our lives have been enriched. We are grateful that beautiful things exist, grateful for the experience they offer us. We call things beautiful when experience of them gives us this particular kind of pleasure. It is a sense that they are as they should be, that there is something exactly right about them.

The problem of taste

We can find things of very different categories beautiful: landscapes, paintings, buildings, works of music, mathematical theorems, pieces of writing. We also have other words with which to try to get at what pleases us: deep, harmonious, fitting, or in less serious contexts, charming, enjoyable, agreeable, neat. The instinct to make things like this is not confined to the great artist or writer. A craftsman may care about it, and so may somebody tidying their desk or choosing a tie. Sometimes, of course, we care about other things than beauty. The orator cares about the impact of his words, and may even be distracted from that goal if he starts putting things too beautifully. Not all successful works, even in the arts, are beautiful. Some are deliberately discordant, or even ugly. Picasso did not, I imagine, intend his protest at the horrors of war, *Guernica*, to be beautiful. Moralists too have often proclaimed that human beauty is only skin deep, a snare and a delusion.

Why does beauty excite philosophical attention? Immanuel Kant pinpointed a paradox, 'the antinomy of taste', that attaches to it. On the one hand, the starting point seems to be our own sensory pleasure. Words like 'charming' or 'boring' seem to report the effect that something has had on us. I properly call something charming only if I have been charmed by it, just as I properly call something boring only if I have been bored by it. In that case we would expect the old motto *de gustibus non est disputandum*, taste is not to be disputed, to hold sway. If I take pleasure in the taste of mint toothpaste and you do not, we do not have to quarrel. I can go my way and you can go yours. It would only be in some unusual or artificial context that we might try to argue about it: for instance, if we are packing for an ultra-lightweight expedition, and only wish to carry one tube. There is no such thing as having the 'right' feeling about mint toothpaste. Whatever seems to you right, is right, and that just means that we cannot talk about right and wrong. It is as if we imagine the image of painting a bullseye wherever your arrow lands and then claiming success in our archery. Perhaps with taste, it is a bit like that. You can't be wrong; you always score 100%.

This is one side of Kant's paradox. The other side is that we care about beauty more than this implies. We do argue about it, and when someone doesn't see things our way, we might get quite hot under the collar. If you and I look at the same thing, and I am ravished and you are not, it can be disturbing, and I may try to convert you. If you cannot see the beauty in the night sky, or you are unmoved by the grandeur of the Alps or the Grand Canyon, the delicacy of the dawn light, or the grace of the child's movements, then we may be quite significantly at odds with one another. These things, I may think, demand such a reaction. At the limit, I may regard your insensitivity as a kind of deformity, putting you down as a boor or a clod: an unfeeling philistine. Of course you in turn might regard me as a queer fish, a sentimentalist or hypersensitive: a mere aesthete. We each regard the other as badly tuned, and contend for our own way of looking at things. That implies that we are prepared to insist on a standard: in our thoughts there is after all such a thing as good taste, as educated judgement, or even as being objectively right or wrong. So it seems that we oscillate between pure subjectivity (*de gustibus* ...) and at least a degree of objectivity.

Beauty matters (so does ugliness)

Furthermore, while we do not often have to agree on which toothpaste to pack, we do need to agree about other things, such as how a building should look, or a city. We envy people who live in beautiful cities and villages, and might reasonably fear that we have lost the art of constructing them. Similarly we fear the loss of beauty in landscapes and wilderness, and the relentless ugly encroachments of concrete and tarmac. And these fears seem somehow much more important than simply the fear of a loss of pleasure. It is more as if something we need, something near to our core, may be vanishing. Hence the formation of preservation societies and the various nostalgias that spill into political action.

Not only do we attach importance to the loss of beautiful things, but also to the loss of our own pleasure in them. Wordsworth laments the decline in the sense of beauty that comes with growing older:

> *There was a time when meadow, grove, and stream,*
> *The earth, and every common sight,*
> *To me did seem*
> *Apparelled in celestial light,*
> *The glory and the freshness of a dream.*
> *It is not now as it hath been of yore; –*
> *Turn wheresoe'er I may*
> *By night or day*
> *The things which I have seen I now can see no more.*

How then are we to reconcile the two sides of Kant's antinomy or paradox? It sounds as though we have to choose between pure objectivity and pure subjectivity. If neither side is completely comfortable, then how can they be harmonized?

We might want to soften the objectivity side a little. It is going a bit far to say that we universally 'demand' the same taste from others. I fear I am not musical enough to appreciate some of the finer beauties of Wagner, but nobody demands that I do. Well-wishers may encourage me to do so, but it is really nobody else's business if I choose not to listen. The fact that a child is reading and exercising their imagination is more important than the content of what they are reading. We may be profoundly shocked to learn that one of the most beautiful paintings in European art, Vermeer's *Girl with a Pearl Earring*, was sold at public auction in The Hague for two guilders in 1881. But it is not shocking in the same way as details of the slave trade or Victorian public school life. We probably think of the people at that auction with a kind of amazement, rather than with outrage or disgust. We also resent people who try to impose their taste more than we resent people who try to impose a moral point of view. With aesthetics, it seems as though we can tolerate more diversity than with ethics.

The subjective or *de gustibus* side of Kant's antinomy needs softening as well. Few things are as undiscussable as the flavour of the toothpaste. A taste for the trite or the sentimental, for chocolate-box pictures and poems, is surely a cause for regret. Art that excites 'cheap' or stereotypical emotions can be offensive, and often we know that it is lying to us, like official art or propaganda. People who have this taste may strike us as childish or lazy or undeveloped, rather like people who can't grow out of train-spotting or playing with soft toys.

No rules

We might try to unearth hidden 'principles' of beauty. But there is something fishy about any such enterprise, and we might expect it to end, as historically all such attempts have done, in failure. Kant pinpoints the reason for scepticism:

There can be no rule according to which anyone is able to be compelled to recognize something as beautiful. Whether a dress, a house, or a flower is beautiful is a matter upon which one declines to allow one's judgement to be swayed by any reasons or principles. We want to get a look at the object with our own eyes.

This is surely right. Rules are to be followed, and if there were 'rules of art' then there would be no room for originality. And, crucially, beauty would not need to be apprehended by the senses. We could just tell each other about it, in the same way that we can describe the layout of a room to someone who has not visited it. But we cannot do this. If someone tells me that a garden or a painting or a wedding was beautiful, but I was not there, then all I can properly say is that I have heard that it was beautiful. I cannot voice the judgement myself. Similarly, if we ask someone whether something is beautiful, they cannot reply in their own voice if they have not experienced it for themselves. I can say that the critics find it beautiful, but I cannot assert that it is so. I may trust the critics, but we use qualified language when we do this: I can say that 'they tell me' it is beautiful, and I can suppose that I ought to go and see it.

On the other hand, we are not simply describing or voicing our own feeling about the object either. I might go to a play, and recognize that it is in fact a very boring play, although I enjoyed myself because one of my children was in the cast. Or, I might recognize that I was 'out of sorts' and therefore took no pleasure in something that was, nevertheless, extremely beautiful. Personal emotions can cloud our appreciation of beauty, and we may know this about ourselves and on occasion discount our own feelings or lack of feelings. We might see someone's beauty, but take no pleasure in it, perhaps through envy or malice. We would understand other people's enchantment, even if for the moment we cannot share it.

The role of the critic

Hence there can be the practice of criticism, in which we try to direct each other's eyes (or ears, or memories) to things that we think may have escaped attention, hidden beauties or blemishes, in the hope of bringing the judgement of others into line with our own. Obviously some people are better at this than others. David Hume isolated a number of qualities needed by the good critic: he must be in a 'sound state', meaning one in which he is receptive to the object in question, have a delicate discrimination, have a practised eye or ear, and at least in literary matters, be a person of good sense and free from prejudice.

That still does not tell us what there is to care about. One suggestion would be that the critic is trying to anticipate or second guess whether the work generally strikes people one way or the other. He would be treating himself as an indicator of the judgements of other people. This was Jean-Jacques Rousseau's view: taste is the faculty of judging what pleases or displeases the greatest number. I would be treating my own reactions as a litmus test, believing myself to be typical enough that my reactions are the ones I can expect to be widely shared. But this theory seems quite wrong. In P.G. Wodehouse's story 'The Episode of the Dog McIntosh', the philistine theatre producer uses his ghastly nine-year-old child as just such a piece of litmus paper: a perfect indicator of the taste of the public. On Rousseau's view we would have to say that the child exhibits excellent taste. As Kant put it, the claim of a judgement of beauty is not that everyone *will* agree with it, but that they *should*. If I say that reality TV shows are disgusting, I am not saying that they disgust most people, since I may know that they do not. I am saying that they should do so, and we may put it by saying that such things demand this reaction. So again we circle back to the problem of subjectivity. Why should we care?

Disappointment

Talk of the beauty of the rose or the night sky as demanding a reaction from us has to be metaphorical. These things make no demands: indeed, one of the things that is part of the beauty of nature or the cosmos may be their vast indifference to the human world. It is only we human beings who make demands on each other.

So what is at stake when we demand a reaction from one another? The language is moral, but what aspect of morality is involved? I once read of a proposal to put a satellite with large reflecting panels into the sky, where it would become a permanent fixture visible in the night hours, and looking about as large as the moon, on which advertisers could project messages. I felt profoundly shocked, shocked to the core by the idea. I felt contaminated just by belonging to a culture in which such a proposal could even be made without the author dying of shame, or being henceforward unable to hold his head up in human company.

In feeling this way, I regarded the night sky as sacred. To me, the idea of putting a large advertising satellite up in it, permanently reflecting Coca Cola or McDonald's advertisements, is not even discussable. We do not have to be conventionally religious to give these things their absolute importance. If someone tramples on them, it would be right to talk of desecration.

Perhaps a better thought is not put in terms of demands, but in terms of disappointment: if you and I visit the Grand Canyon, and I am blown away, and you are merely bored, I will be disappointed in you. A gulf has opened up between us. As I suggested above, I may have the idea that this is a kind of deformity in you; a lack of something necessary to make people fully human, and similarly with the night sky.

I might put it by saying that you don't care enough, or care in the right way. And I think this begins to point towards a solution to Kant's paradox. Someone blind to beauty cannot be taken out of himself; perhaps cannot forget his or her own concerns, cannot pause or enlarge his or her gaze. Appreciating beauty, we concentrate upon the object itself, but there is no limit to the thoughts it engenders. Beauty catalyses the free play of the imagination. It does not direct us to think one thing or the other, which is why we are so typically lost for words in its presence. As Kant put it,

> By an aesthetic idea I mean that representation of the imagination which induces much thought, yet without the possibility of any definite thought whatever being adequate to it.

Beauty can be seen as clearing the decks, as it were, towards an appreciation of other things, of the world, of things apart from ourselves and our own limited concerns. The beauty of a wilderness speaks of the greatness of nature and the smallness of human beings; the beauty of a rural landscape speaks of the care and attention of generations of people who have cared for it; the beauty of the rose speaks of the fleeting nature of pleasure and the acceptance of mortality. These things refresh our spirits, and this is what we feel when we gaze at them, however dumb we are struck.

I think we are right to be disappointed in people who seem unable to find this kind of significance in their experience. We may even be suspicious of them, as Shakespeare was:

> *The man that has no music in himself*
> *Nor is not moved with concord of sweet sounds*
> *Is fit for treasons, stratagems and spoils;*
> *The motions of his spirit are as dull as night,*
> *And affections dark as Erebus:*
> *Let no such man be trusted.*

The philistine is a concern to us because he cannot be taken out of himself. He cannot share our imaginings. He is a danger, as we see when he controls the built environment, or the stewardship of nature. He is especially a danger when he presides over the commodification of humanities, arts, sciences and education, each to be put entirely at the service of an 'economic' model, made to justify themselves at the bar of gross national product. This deformity of political thinking is not a new development: as far back as 1795 the same fear was voiced by the great German poet and aesthetic theorist Friedrich Schiller in his *Letters on the Education of Mankind*:

> *In our day it is necessity, neediness, that prevails, and bends a degraded humanity under its iron yoke. Utility is the great idol of the time, to which all powers do homage and all subjects are subservient. In this great balance of utility, the spiritual service of art has no weight, and, deprived of all encouragement, it vanishes from the noisy Vanity Fair of our time.*

It is perhaps with education that we see the moral element of appreciation of beauty most clearly. When no time is left for the free play of the imagination, but learning is a matter of drudgery and repetition, its success measured only by economic ends of which the child has no comprehension, how should we expect any more than a sullen rejection, a rebellion against everything that school and the adult world represent? The reality is that our economic activities ought to be at the service of truth and beauty, not the other way around.

By taking us out of ourselves beauty reminds us of all this. This is why its experience does not present itself as a 'mere' pleasure, a momentary titillation. We know that in some profound way it connects with the deeper or spiritual side of life. In other words, by enrapturing us, it reminds us of the most important and enduring elements of our world and our human place in it.

Do We Need God?
Hope, consolation and judgement

Several chapters in this work contribute to the question of the existence of God, but it is important enough to justify pulling the strands together. For some people believe that it is life's great question: the axle on which the wheels of spirituality, meaning, values and hope all turn.

Others think it opens up nothing but fantasy and myth, the dreams and fictions with which some people unfortunately seem to embellish their world. The truth, I shall argue, is more subtle.

Some arguments

I shall start by briefly rehearsing where David Hume leaves religion at the end of his great *Dialogues Concerning Natural Religion*. In this work there are three principal characters. The first is Philo, a religious sceptic, whose voice is clearly that of Hume himself. Cleanthes is an apologist whose stock-in-trade is the argument to design for the existence of a deity, the familiar argument that the delicate and wonderful adjustments of nature irresistibly point to the existence of a divine architect: all nature declares the Creator's glory. Finally there is Demea, who wants the God of the philosophers: infinite, perfect, immutable, eternal or transcending space and time, incomprehensible and mysterious. Demea could have been modelled on Gottfried Wilhelm Leibniz, whose 'cosmological argument', which attempts to arrive at God from bare consideration of the question why there is something and not nothing, we have already visited (see *Why Is There Something and Not Nothing?*).

Cleanthes presents himself as a reasonable, scientific kind of thinker. His divine architect is going to be the natural conclusion of a piece of scientific reasoning, just like that which has us believe, when we find a watch, that it was created by a watchmaker. Unfortunately this analogy, the darling of religious apologists in the centuries following Newton's revelation of order in nature, and in our own time the stock-in-trade of 'intelligent design', runs into well-known problems.

First, our own creative activities are highly dependent on the delicate adjustments of the physical world. Our brains are even more delicately adjusted, more complex, more marvellous than our watches. So if we postulate design to explain complexity, and we want to rely upon an analogy with the human design of human artefacts, we are really only postulating something yet more complex than what we set out to explain.

Second, human designers need stuff to make things from, whereas God is supposed to have made everything out of nothing. Third, our ideas are ideas of the things we come across in that world. We do not have thoughts in a vacuum, but in response to sense experience, and we express them using language with which we cope with our world. But none of these things is true of the Divine Architect, who has to pluck materials and ideas out of nowhere. Fourth, human designers are dependent on parents, not self-caused or self-explaining. So are we to posit an infinite line of gods, each responsible for the next? Fifth, in a particularly nice move, Hume points out that our aims and our passions are adapted to the animal and social lives we lead. As evolutionary psychologists like to remind us, emotions such as fear or anger are adaptations to frightening circumstances, or social circumstances that we want to reject and change. That cannot be true of the Divine Architect. He is not supposed to inhabit any particular ecological niche at all.

Illusion and design

The inference from a watch to a watchmaker is good because we know that this is how watches get made, and we also know a lot about the process and materials that the watchmaker relies upon. We know nothing of the sort when it comes to the existence of universes.

In fact, the argument to design is so bad that it is tempting to look for an explanation of its enduring appeal. I believe that underneath it lies the same illusion that leads people to an 'interventionist' conception of free will (see *Am I Free?*). In our day-to-day doings we are unconscious of the myriad causal structures in our brains and bodies that underlie and sustain our actions. This tempts us to think that in our own agency we have an example of an uncaused will, and this in turn leads us to sympathy with the idea of a mind that does not need a body or brain or physical nature, or even a location, but which nevertheless does things. So design becomes a plausible explanation of the cosmos. Once we firmly understand that human design is just a small local productive principle located within the cosmos, and is utterly and completely dependent on physically complex structures within the cosmos, the illusion should lose its grip.

The fact that a cosmos designer would itself inhabit no ecological niche clearly makes it impossible for us to do any more than guess at what might motivate him, if anything does. The great naturalist J.B.S. Haldane is reported to have thought long and hard when asked what we might infer about the desires and values of the deity from the wonderful course of nature, and eventually replied: 'he seems to have an inordinate fondness for beetles' (of which there are something like half a million species, compared to our one). Perhaps that is as far as we can speculate.

But suppose we waive those difficulties, we still have it that human designers work in groups, refine the designs of others, sometimes lose interest in their designs, go on to make improved versions, and so on. Cleanthes' theology leaves it open that the world

> for aught he knows, is very faulty and imperfect, compared to a superior standard; and was only the first rude essay of some infant deity, who afterwards abandoned it, ashamed of his lame performance: it is the work only of some dependent, inferior deity; and is the object of derision to his superiors: it is the production of old age and dotage in some superannuated deity; and ever since his death, has run on at adventures, from the first impulse and active force which it received from him.

And Philo rightly concludes that 'I cannot, for my part, think that so wild and unsettled a theology is, in any respect, preferable to none at all.'

Little better than an atheist

The irony is that Demea agrees to all this: when it comes down to it, Cleanthes' anthropomorphic conception of God (one modelled on human beings) leaves him no better than an atheist! But then when we turn to Demea's theology it turns out to be host to yet more difficulties, as we saw when discussing Leibniz's cosmological argument (see *Why Is There Something and Not Nothing?*). In a nutshell, Demea's version of the deity is one that is left completely incomprehensible. Cleanthes in turn retorts that 'belief' in something of which you have absolutely no understanding at all, Demea's mysticism, is *itself* little better than atheism! If I ask you what is in a box, it makes no difference whether you say there is nothing there, or there is something there shut off from human eyes, mysterious, incomprehensible, beyond space and time, but perfect. The second assertion is longer, but boils down to the same thing.

We could put it by saying that the anthropomorphic conception of the deity needs an injection of the mystical in order to avoid the feeble conclusions that are left by the argument to design. But the mystical conception needs a dose of anthropomorphism, to make its deity relevant to human beings. So Hume has the two wings of theology both needing each other, and yet at systematic loggerheads.

Philo, or Hume, then makes a surprising move. He says that since this is so, the difference between all parties is merely verbal.

That sounds extraordinary to most people. They think that the question of the existence of the deity is one of the most important there can be. How could anyone say that the issue is merely verbal? Well, Philo the sceptic says that we cannot understand or know anything about any transcendent reality that explains or sustains the ongoing order of nature. The theist like Demea says that we cannot understand or know anything about the transcendent reality, *which is God*, that explains or sustains the ongoing order of nature. Since the inserted clause does not add anything except a word, the difference between them is merely verbal, as Hume concludes. He even thinks we can, if we wish, speculate that whatever causes or sustains the ongoing order of nature may bear some remote analogy to other forces that make things happen within nature, human design amongst them.

This, incidentally, probably explains why Hume never described himself as an atheist. The atheist and the theist collude in thinking that there is something definite to argue about, an issue about which one side says 'yes' and the other says 'no'. But this is just what Hume denies. Indeed, at the end of the *Dialogues*, the little boy, Pamphilius, who is present as an auditor, says that Cleanthes' arguments appealed to him the most, and even Philo, surprisingly, makes some apparently complimentary remarks about the design argument, provided it has a completely undefined conclusion. Some commentators have rather flat-footedly thought that this was some kind of recantation on Hume's part. But it wasn't. If you are stuck without any usable conception of a deity, it should matter not in the least whether you are drawn to say that 'it' exists or to deny it. There is no inference to be drawn about anything – moral, political, empirical or theoretical – from either the assertion that 'it' does exist or the atheist assertion that 'it' does not exist. Joining in on either side equally implies that we know what we are talking about, and the right philosophical attitude is just to laugh at persons who suppose that.

Beliefs and practices

I believe this analysis is decisive, if the question is one of belief. But suppose religion only *disguises* itself as a matter of believing anything? We raised the question of why there is something rather than nothing and tried to dispel the sense of mystery surrounding it (see *Why Is There Something and Not Nothing?*). We also met Schopenhauer's explanation of the relentless appeal to the question, in our need to confront our own mortality. Now, having located the drive in our emotional natures, Schopenhauer did not think it would just go away, or that it would be a good thing if it did. He thought that the metaphysical drive would continue for ever to nurture the flight to religions, which weave their myths around the blank in our understanding:

> *Before the people truth cannot appear naked. A symptom of this allegorical nature of religions is the mysteries, to be found perhaps in every religion, that is, certain dogmas that cannot even be distinctly conceived, much less be literally true . . . these are the only suitable way of making the ordinary mind and uncultured understanding feel what would be incomprehensible to it, namely that religion deals at bottom with an entirely different order. . . In the presence of such an order the laws of this phenomenal world, according to which it must speak, disappear.*

Schopenhauer's view here fits nicely with the position in which Alice is left at one point in *Alice Through the Looking Glass*. Alice reads to herself the marvellous nonsense poem 'Jabberwocky' – ''Twas brillig, and the slithy toves / Did gyre and gimble in the wabe . . .':

> *'It seems very pretty,' she said when she had finished it, 'but it's rather hard to understand' (you see she didn't like to confess, even to herself, that she couldn't make it out at all). 'Somehow it seems to fill my head with ideas – only I don't exactly know what they are!'*

Suppose a person is left in the grip of Schopenhauer's emotional desire to confront his own mortality. He confronts the riddle of existence, and suppose then he does come back with his head oscillating between mystical and anthropomorphic imaginings. He has, let us say, a God that is beyond space and time, but that in the next breath comes down to earth; a perfect God who made a rotten world; a God who is unchanging, but who also gets angry and disappointed; a being unlike us, and yet jealous and pleased by expensive enough sacrifices; a God only to be described in contradictory terms, or perhaps approached by inadequate metaphors and analogies. These imaginings may be too vague and too unstable to deserve calling real belief in anything. But they can do other things.

For a start, they may predispose a person to want guidance from other people, who with less self-knowledge or more self-confidence claim to have seen further, and in particular to have seen moral and practical injunctions issuing from the divine mist (in just the same way that Tenniel's drawing of a Jabberwock set the imaginations of generations of Lewis Carroll's readers). If a forceful enough person claims that his or her revelation has cut through the darkness of our understanding, and lo and behold, the deity has told him various things to do and not to do, there will be a temptation to hold his hand, to escape from the intolerable burden of darkness into what is promised to be light. And so people tumble into cults and faiths, cemented together with rituals, sacrifices, myths and above all promises. None of it makes sense, but none of it has to make sense to work its effects, for good or ill.

In this account, paradox and contradiction thus become not so much objections to the complicated states of mind that religions engender, but a central part of them. This is actually not entirely unorthodox: there is a wing of theology, called the *via negativa* or apophatic tradition, which rejoices in the fact that we can understand nothing about God. This tradition is more prominent in Buddhism and some Islamic schools than it is in religions that set more store by dogma, such as Judaism or Christianity. The distinguished economist Amartya Sen relates that when he told his grandfather that he was an atheist, the old man replied that this was very good, since it meant he had joined the Lokayata tradition of Hinduism!

Human graffiti

The upshot is that there is something misleading in talking of 'religious belief' as simply another kind of belief, or 'religious truth' as another kind of truth. In ordinary contexts a 'belief' that, say, there are some people in the room and no people in the room, is not a belief at all. A belief is a guide towards acting in the world, but anyone saying such a sentence, contradicting themselves, has no guide to hand. The machinery is just whirring; the gears are not engaged. The same ought to be just as true of theological contradictions. The early church father Tertullian is supposed to have said 'Credo quia impossibile est' (I believe because it is impossible), irritating generations of logicians and philosophers who reply that if it is impossible, then it cannot be true, and if you know that, either you cannot believe it or you certainly ought not to. But Schopenhauer enables us to see why it does not work like that.

Faced with a blank wall, many emotions will tempt people to scribble their own graffiti on it, or gratefully accept the graffiti of others. So we get myths and authorities, people licensed to draw on the wall. A myth is a personification of collective fantasies, fears and desires. So we have stories of gods sharing human suffering, of gods dispensing the justice that is not found here on earth, of gods that prefer us to our neighbours, of gods that can be propitiated by the right sacrifices or by growing the right facial hair or wearing the right hats, of gods more merciful than the world in which we have found ourselves, or who dispense a fiercer justice to the wicked than any that is found on earth.

Opponents of religious practice like to enumerate the bad things that may come of all this: persecutions, wars, denial of rights, oppression of those who are supposed to be less in the good books of the deity. These are common knowledge. More subtle are the distortions and hypocrisies that come when a sensible, humane decency becomes displaced by an emphasis on the virtues of particular practices, or the importance of belonging to one cult or another.

On the other side there is good evidence from social science that societies held together by some kind of religious practice do better than ones which are not. Some studies suggest that a group which splits off from the mainstream, and tries to set itself up as a self-sustaining commune, is likely to last about four times as long if it has such a practice than if it does not. Perhaps we are evolutionarily adapted to need shared rituals and sayings when the need for metaphysics comes over us. But there are other more tangible benefits as well. Imaginings of invisible agents can play a role in cementing cooperative social behaviour, and therefore benefit any groups of people who are prone to such imaginings. There is ample experimental evidence of effects like this. Very young children told that an invisible princess is in the room watching them are less likely to open a forbidden box. College students who have been casually told that the experimental room is sometimes said to be haunted by the ghost of a dead student proved less likely to cheat on a task they had been set, in a situation that made cheating possible. And experimental subjects who have been 'primed' even by casual exposure to sentences involving terms like 'God' and 'sacred' are more likely to make cooperative offers to partners in various economic games.

Finally, we can remember the nice real-life example of a similar effect (see *Why Be Good?*). This was the problem where those taking coffee or tea were supposed to put in amounts of money pinned up on a small piece of paper beside the dispenser, but were not doing so nearly enough. A quite small heading on the notice showing a pair of eyes looking straight at the viewer resulted in nearly three times as much money paid in as in weeks where the notice had no such picture on it, but only a neutral image of flowers.

It seems, then, that poor old humanity is sufficiently dysfunctional that it takes imaginary witnesses, ghosts, and invisible agencies to keep us in order. Perhaps we ought to be grateful to the writers and artists, storytellers and charismatics who have given us our myths, provided we remember that that is what they are.

What is it All For?
The pursuit of the meaning of life

There is no shortage of answers to this question. Pleasure, happiness, contentment, loving, being loved, keeping busy, knowledge, power, achievement, doing good, knowing God, wisdom, reproduction and not asking silly questions are just a few of them.

It is worth separating two directions in which people look for the meaning of life. One is beyond life itself. We are to fix our gaze and our hopes on another world, another way of being, which is free from the mess and sorrow, the frantic motions and events of present life. Our insignificance in this cosmos is compensated by assurance of significance in a wider scheme of things. There is hope in another world. In this picture the source of meaning transcends the ordinary mundane world of our bounded lives and bounded visions. The literature, art, music and practices of religion are then thought to give voice to this attitude to meaning. The attitudes are only possible if we pin our faith on a world beyond. Many people would call this the spiritual option, but I shall suggest that this is to kidnap a good word for a doubtful purpose. Instead, since we are to transcend the small, squalid, contingent, finite, animal nature of earthly existence, we can call this the *transcendental* option.

The transcendental option can give people hope, when they find that their hopes in this life are unfulfilled. Humanity's bitter world often seems aptly modelled in the myth of Sisyphus, the King of Corinth punished by the gods by being forced perpetually to roll a boulder up a hill, only to have it break loose as he neared the top and roll back to the bottom again. In this world people's hopes are often betrayed, their lives end in failure, their delights turn to ashes. These moralistic clichés encourage a turn to the transcendental, the timeless world where there is no decay, no death, no disappointment or despair. Apparent success only paints a fig leaf over disaster: in Voltaire's satire *Candide*, even the optimistic doctor Pangloss acknowledges as much:

> 'Human grandeur,' said Pangloss, 'is very dangerous, if we believe the testimonies of almost all philosophers; for we find Eglon, King of Moab, was assassinated by Aod; Absalom was hanged by the hair of his head, and run through with three darts; King Nadab, son of Jeroboam, was slain by Baaza; King Ela by Zimri; Okosias by Jehu; Athaliah by Jehoiada; the Kings Jehooiakim, Jeconiah, and Zedekiah, were led into captivity: I need not tell you what was the fate of Croesus, Astyages, Darius, Dionysius of Syracuse, Pyrrhus, Perseus, Hannibal, Jugurtha, Ariovistus, Caesar, Pompey, Nero, Otho, Vitellius, Domitian, Richard II of England, Edward II, Henry VI, Richard III, Mary Stuart, Charles I, the three Henrys of France, and the Emperor Henry IV.'

In spite of this depressing theme, the opposite option is to look for meaning only within life itself. This is the *immanent* option.

It is content with the everyday. There is sufficient meaning for human beings in the human world – the world of familiar, and even humdrum, doings and experiences. In the immanent option, the smile of the baby, the grace of the dancer, the sound of voices, the movement of a lover, even the passing of light and shadow or the murmur of the sea, give meaning to life. For some it is activity and achievement: gaining the summit of the mountain, crossing the finishing line first or writing the poem. These things last only their short time, but that does not deny them meaning. A smile does not need to go on forever in order to mean what it does. There is nothing beyond or apart from the processes of life. Furthermore, there is no one goal to which all these processes tend, but we can find something precious – value and meaning – in the processes themselves. There is no such thing as *the* meaning of life, but there can be many meanings within a life. Hence the torrent of potential answers with which I started.

Scale

An attractive variant of the second option opens up when we think slightly more generously of the width of our concerns. Suppose I do not so much wish for things for myself, but aim at a larger goal: improving a medicine, or perfecting a process, or putting my university or school or town or club on the map. Then if these things come about partly as a result of my efforts, even after my death, they could be said to have given my life meaning. I shall not necessarily be around to say that, but others can say it of me. Unfortunately there is a downside, which is that if these things do not come about, and perhaps had no significant chance of coming about, others may talk of a wasted life, a futile pursuit which had no good outcome. This is sometimes so, but not always.

We might think it is always so: looking at the way in which the world goes on, the infinitesimal difference even our best efforts make, and only for an insignificant time on one insignificant planet in an insignificant galaxy, we may all feel condemned to futility. But as Frank Ramsey, a great (and rather large) Cambridge philosopher of the early 20th century, said:

> *Where I seem to differ from my friends is in attaching little importance to physical size. I don't feel in the least humble before the vastness of the heavens. The stars may be large, but they cannot think or love; and these are qualities which impress me far more than size does. I take no credit for weighing nearly seventeen stone. My picture of the world is drawn in perspective, and not like a model to scale. The foreground is occupied by human beings and the stars are all as small as threepenny bits.*

There are lives which are by no means futile, in the human scale. In this scale Beethoven's life, or Einstein's, or that of Salk who invented the polio vaccine or James Watt who invented the steam engine had meaning, as do millions of others in less dramatic ways. We may be 'poor players that strut and fret our hour upon the stage', but we can do things to leave the stage just a little better than we found it, and that may give meaning to our lives. This too is an immanent option, but not a selfish one or a materialistic one.

If we go around galleries of western European art we find a profound change from early in the 17th century. Before that most art gave expression to a transcendental yearning. Medieval religious art depicts the promise of heaven or the horrors of hell, the terrible dramas of God become incarnate and sharing our sufferings here on earth, the dramas of resurrection and salvation. From around 1600, in Spain and then especially in the Netherlands, we find more of the everyday. For the first time there are still lives, depicting ordinary domestic objects in ordinary domestic settings (the writer André Gide talked of still lives as portraying 'the silent life of objects'). Portraits loosen their connection with saints and with religious and royal offices, and become more intimate, more homely, more concerned with everyday life and appearance. It is as if a long love affair with the transcendental is finally growing tired, and being replaced by a celebration of the here and now. There had been paintings of everyday life before, but often with a moralistic edge to them, as ships of fools sink to the bottom, or inebriated peasants neglect their business. Beauty had to come in the face of the virgin, or under the legitimizing clothing of ancient mythology. But quietly, and slowly, the everyday reasserted itself. In painters like Vermeer the most homely activities and homely scenes become infused with a weight, a dignity and a significance that was previously reserved for the mysteries of the church.

Some philosophers argue that this change was not so much from a religious to a secular world view, as from one religion to another. They interpret the gradual onset of the modern world as the substitution of a gospel of progress for a gospel of renunciation. But that is not in general true. There have indeed been thinkers with a gospel of progress: optimists who thought that with education or science or the decline of religious fanaticism, eras of peace and prosperity were just around the corner. Few believe that at the beginning of the 21st century. But we might immerse ourselves in the day-to-day business of living, or we might aim for a result that improves things for our fellow countrymen, or for human beings in general, or even for other animals, without having much confidence in a gospel of progress in general.

Spiritual experiences

Some people find themselves pointing in a transcendental direction and some in one of the immanent directions. I suspect this is not a matter of deliberate choice, but more a matter of temperament and experience, aided and abetted by the surrounding culture and accidents of education. Some are more comfortable in the everyday world than others, but many lives have few or no moments of either dignity or tranquillity, and for those living them the consolations of belief in something higher may prove irresistible. In moments of despair and desolation the belief that this is all that there is may be hard to bear.

But equally, transcendental hopes may well strike us as nothing but wish-fulfilment, fiction and delusion: as we put it in the last chapter, they are human graffiti scribbled on the blank wall we face when we attempt to come to terms with our own deaths. And there is surely something self-defeating about imagining a transcendental world modelled on this one, yet whose existence would give meaning to this one, as if we could grasp a mode of being that would not, at the bottom, just be more of the same. Things do not gain meaning just by going on for a very long time, or even forever. Indeed, they lose it. A piece of music, a conversation, even a glance of adoration or a moment of unity with another person have their allotted time. Too much and they become boring. An infinity and they would be intolerable. Yet if the transcendental world is vaguely assumed to be 'timeless' then we have to ask if we understand the difference between timeless existence and extinction, and I think the answer has to be that there is none. Time conditions all our imaginings (see *Does Time Go By?*).

Centuries of propaganda have left many people vaguely guilty about taking the immanent option. It is stigmatized as 'materialistic' or 'unspiritual'. Professional cheerleaders for the transcendental option use every device they can to demean it. The mistake here is to allow the transcendental option to monopolize everything good or deep about the notion of spirituality. A piece of music or a great painting, or simply the sight of a dolphin in the sea or a hawk in the sky, can allow us a respite from everyday concerns, or give us the occasion for uses of the imagination that expand our range of sympathy and understanding. They indeed take us out of ourselves. But they do not do so by taking us to somewhere else. The imagination they unlock, or the sentiments and feelings they inspire, still belong to this world. In the best cases, it is this world only now seen less egocentrically, seen without our own problems being at the centre of it. Such experiences deserve to be called spiritual, although the word may have suffered so much from its religious captivity that it cannot be said without embarrassment. Fortunately, the phenomena it describes do not die with it.

And sacred causes

The same strictures might be said about religious appropriation of the idea of something sacred. To regard something as sacred is to see it as marking a boundary to what may be done. Something is regarded as sacred when it is not to be sacrificed to other things, not to be weighed in a cost-benefit analysis, not to be touched. The memory of a loved one is sacred when it is not to be questioned or assessed. The scientist says that truth is sacred when he regards deception, or even just inaccuracy, as shocking, and regards the idea that we might go in for a bit of it, say, for financial gain, undiscussable. We do not need to move into religious territory to voice the idea of something being sacred.

We saw a particularly clear example in which a mere matter of taste (the beauty of the night sky) became a moral issue (see *What Is Beauty?*). The problem with the proposal to desecrate it with an advertising logo is its insensitivity and willingness to impose. It would deny everyone the range of emotions that the night sky properly calls for, including awe and wonder, perhaps fear, perhaps consolation. In spite of Ramsey's celebration of the human perspective, there is something valuable about the way in which the size of the cosmos puts us in our place. To destroy that would be the equivalent at least of playing loud and often unwanted music everywhere, all the time. It would be denying people a solace they want, and that is a crime against humanity. We may call it a crime against the night sky, but I see that as shorthand for what is really going wrong. The cosmos is big enough to take the odd McDonald's advertisement, but we are not.

If I think the night sky is to be treated as untouchable, and feel profoundly shocked and despondent at the idea of commercial exploitation of it, then I cannot respect those who feel otherwise. We have an issue. Nor can we agree to differ, for in practice that amounts to letting them have their way, if they can raise the money or interest the sponsors. I have to oppose them, and this is what is meant by saying that it is a moral issue. I have to hold that they are wrong. Having the wrong attitudes is here as bad or worse than having the wrong beliefs. Of course it may be that I cannot prove (to them) that they are wrong. They may think I am being sentimental or over-sensitive, and then we have to argue, by drawing on analogies and other cases, by trying to turn their minds around. The process may or may not be successful. There are few quick victories in moral discussions, but the stakes are too high to abandon the field, and all we can do is to soldier on.

At the beginning of the 17th century, the transcendental option began to give way to the immanent option. At the beginning of the 21st century, there is little sign of any celebration of the everyday in our art and writing. There are no Vermeers amongst us any more. Contemporary film and writing is seldom a celebration of anything, but more likely to dwell on images of catastrophe and doom, the decline of civilization, the coming of the night. Perhaps this mood is justified, but whether or not things are going to be better or worse or just the same in the future, it certainly makes life even more miserable than it needs to be in the present. So perhaps instead of thinking so much about the future, we should indeed immerse ourselves in the present. After all, at the end of his satire Voltaire has the hero who has experienced all the horrors of life and tried mightily to understand them, conclude with the advice, 'Let us cultivate our garden.' Human beings are built to live in the present, so perhaps the path of wisdom, and the best the philosopher can advise, is that we remember to do so.

What are My Rights?
Positive, negative and natural rights

The question, 'What are my rights?' might be asked simply as a point of information, meaning, 'What may I do according to the rules of some association or some body politic, and where are the rules are written down or understood?'

I may have the right to bring one guest in, but not two, or the right to walk the pavement, but not to obstruct it. Different rights may be accorded to different people: a citizen may have the right to vote in an election, but not a foreign visitor. My rights are here a matter of what the rules permit.

Nonsense on stilts?

It is not too difficult to see how societies evolve systems of permissions on the one hand and boundaries that must not be crossed on the other. If I have carefully made a bow and arrow then others may protect me in my intention to use it, and institute disapproval and punishment against you who try to take it away from me. If a man and woman claim a status meaning that they are paired together, then it may become a crime, in the eyes of the society, for a third party to ignore the status and try to muscle in. Even among animals, signals can change a status, such that the pack will turn on an animal that then abuses that status (see *Is There Such a Thing as Society?*). We can thus understand the evolution of systems of promise-giving and keeping, systems of property, and eventually systems of law. Where we have these things we have different 'positive' rights, meaning systems of boundaries and permissions, and systems of status that mean that others must forbear from behaving in various ways. All of these are social constructions, in the sense that they owe their existence to the actions and habits of the society.

Things become more problematic if we talk not of rights that owe their existence to these systems, but of 'natural' rights; rights that just exist anyway. Philosophers have sometimes doubted whether such talk even makes sense, any more than talk of natural systems of traffic regulation or natural political systems make sense. They find talk of rights in this second sense too abstract and too uncontrolled to be of genuine use in moral and political discussions. Criticizing the Declaration of Rights issued during the French Revolution, the legal theorist and philosopher Jeremy Bentham famously said that 'natural rights is simply nonsense: natural and imprescriptible rights, rhetorical nonsense – nonsense upon stilts.' The revolutionaries had claimed to expound the 'natural, sacred, and inalienable rights of man', and the horrible course of the revolution itself was still fresh in people's minds when Bentham wrote. According to Bentham, the adjective 'right', as in 'right thing to do' or 'right decision', was fine:

It is in this shape that, passing in at the heart, it gets posses-
sion of the understanding: it then assumes its substantive

*shape, and joining itself to a band of suitable associates, sets
up the banner of insurrection, anarchy, and lawless violence.*

In other words, as soon as it becomes a noun and people start to
talk about 'rights' everything goes pear-shaped:

> *Right, the substantive right, is the child of law: from real laws
> come real rights; but from imaginary laws, from laws of nature,
> fancied and invented by poets, rhetoricians, and dealers in
> moral and intellectual poisons, come imaginary rights, a bas-
> tard brood of monsters, 'gorgons and chimaeras dire'.*

Descriptive or prescriptive?

Natural rights can certainly sound strange, and perhaps a hang-
over from some idea of humanity as forming a kind of 'natural'
community, perhaps one whose rules had been ordained by a
divinity. Each of us would have been born with a set of permissions and privileges inscribed in our genes, so to speak. If we
wish to extend the notion to other species, as animal liber-
ationists do, or even to other things in the natural world, as 'deep'
ecologists sometimes do, then animals, trees, rivers and moun-
tains would be thought of as having a similar inscription. It does
not take too much scepticism to doubt whether such notions
make any kind of sense, or could possibly have any kind of use.

We may reasonably fear the uncontrolled expansion of
rights that this talk encourages. It is bad enough in the human
world. Do people have the right to a job, paid holidays, a particular standard of living, freedom from fear or annoyance or

offence? Does freedom of religion include freedom to bring your children up indoctrinated with any kind of nonsense, or to deny them medical treatment when they need it? And if we go to the natural world, it becomes even worse. Do bacteria have rights? Is eradicating the smallpox virus something akin to genocide? If the Colorado River has a right to reach the sea, then does it also have a right not to be dammed, or indeed drunk at all? Even if we draw back from this unbridled expansion we may regret the adversarial colour of discussions conducted in terms of rights. Rights claims seem peculiarly adapted to generate heat: 'I know my rights' is the kind of remark that one hears, in one's imagining, as uttered with a red face and a fist thumping the table. It does not seem conducive to harmonious, cooperative attempts to find political and moral solutions, and this too was a criticism mounted by Bentham, and later by Karl Marx.

Although these criticisms are important, I do not think they are decisive. We have already identified positive rights in terms of social systems and their structures of boundaries, permissions and privileges. Additionally, it is surely in order to talk of rights as part of a demand that the rules be changed to bear on people differently than they now do. Perhaps the law currently allows you to fly your aircraft over my house to the airport just beyond at any time of day or night. I may protest at the noise nuisance, complaining that it infringes on my right to a good night's sleep. It may not be a part of the established law that things should be ordered so that I can get a good night's sleep. But, I complain, it ought to be. There ought to be a law against the night flying. My rights are being infringed. I am talking about what ought to be the case, not what is the case, and the claim to a right seems to be a good way of doing this.

Suppose I am a democrat. I firmly believe that people who belong to the society should have an equal voice in how that society is run. I hold that there is something very wrong about political systems that deny those affected by political decisions the opportunity to have an equal voice in the making of those decisions. Surely I ought to be able to express these views by saying that people have a right to participate in the democratic process, and that their rights are infringed if some confederacy fails to give them the ability to participate, or snatches it away from them? I am here *prescribing* what positive rights people in societies should be allocated, rather than *describing* some mysterious menu that nature has given them at birth.

We should see talk of natural rights as part of the vocabulary of advocacy, and this is presumably a large part of the way the poor and downtrodden saw it at the time of the French Revolution. In this spirit, even the right of the river to reach the sea is not too metaphysical to stomach. The activist proclaiming it is simply advocating that people must refrain from arranging their affairs so that the river stops short of the sea. That may, or may not, be a good thing to advocate. Most of us are probably happiest when our rivers do reach the sea; on the other hand, all of us depend upon water to drink, and may have to take it out of the rivers around us.

Generalizations and grounds

Bentham's fundamental complaint against the French Declaration of Rights was that its highly abstract language was supposed by itself to provide sufficient reason to overturn an established political order:

> *Hasty generalization, the great stumbling-block of intellec-tual vanity! Hasty generalization, the rock that even genius itself is so apt to split upon! Hasty generalization, the bane of prudence and of science!*

Once it could be said that a government infringed the people's right to liberty or to equality, then, according to the revolution-aries, this gave a sufficient justification for insurrection and for overturning it in favour of something else. But any government can be seen to infringe against 'rights' couched in such an abstract way. Many laws restrict liberties, although not all; many offices such as that of a magistrate or tax collector introduce inequality, since such an office distinguishes between things that some may do and others may not. A magistrate can impose a sentence, and a tax collector demand money with menaces. A private citizen may not. Bentham saw this kind of political language as nothing better than an invitation to anarchy, which under the pretence of giving everyone a right to everything ensured instead that the idea of an enforceable right collapsed, and nobody had any rights at all.

The remedy, however, need not be to ditch the language of rights altogether, but to be a good deal more careful to specify which rights are to be protected and the extent and the limits of the protections thus granted. The history of actual law in mature societies shows the constant evolution of this process. In its nat-ural course, rights may ebb and flow: in Britain as I write there is considerable unrest over the careless extension of the powers of the state to pry and snoop and imprison and generally intrude, all in the name of combating terrorism. This is, of course, the stuff of politics, and there is no reason why advocates of different policies should not use the language of rights to advance their views.

Things become philosophically harder if rights are thought to explain *why* policies are to be advocated. Someone may thus claim that the reason why, say, the state should not censor some kind of material is that people have a right to choose it. Or, they may say, we must arrange our affairs democratically *because* people have the right to participate in the political process. Here the right seems to be thought of as grounding the policy being urged. And this seems to bring us back to the metaphysically queer idea of the right as some kind of fact to which we can appeal, a ground for a policy rather than simply a term used in advocating the policy. It sounds as though we must be drawn back to the mysterious menu inscribed on each of us at birth.

Weighing and trumping

This is not, however, necessarily so. We might explain why we are advocating a policy by invoking a right, without playing into the hands of the sceptic about the whole notion. We would do this if we showed how the policy accorded with already recognized and established rights, and of course much legal and political argument takes exactly that form. An advertisement, for instance, might be defended on the grounds of an advertiser's right to free speech, or opposed on the ground of a public's right to protection against fraud. Each side can say that it is *because* their policy accords with some established right that it should prevail.

This would be staying within the sphere of established or settled, positive rights. It is what the Supreme Court in the United States sets itself to do, scrutinizing the language of the Constitution with the most minute and pedantic care and a huge battery of previous interpretations to draw upon. As Bentham predicted, the result can often be laughable from the standpoint of the good of society. There is nothing to stop the 18th-century 'right of the people to bear arms', which in context clearly referred to their right to form militias in defence of the country, from including the right of any individual to own 20th-century assault weapons, and no doubt bombs, poison gases and tactical nuclear weapons if such become available. The method is essentially the scholastic one of poring over the meaning of a sacred text, and other considerations, such as a people's right to have their government protect their safety, seem, at least from the outside, to be completely forgotten in the process.

It would be nice for moral theory if some highly general and undeniable fact about human beings legitimized at least some entries on their menu of natural rights. Historically the most promising candidate has been our shared rationality. The attempt would be to show that because we are conscious, deliberating, choosing animals, any legitimate society must include principles guaranteeing various kinds of freedom. Liberalism, in its philosophical aspect, might be seen as an attempt to articulate just such a route, first putting our acknowledged capacities into the hat, and then drawing out a budget of things to which we each have a right, such as freedom of expression, freedom of religion, freedom under the law, the right to a fair trial, or in other words freedom from unfair coercion by the law and freedom to participate in the political process. In the work of the most eminent liberal theorist of the 20th century, John Rawls, the bare structure of the legitimate state could be derived from the idea that it could rationally be chosen by free agents, contracting together to choose the rules under which they would cooperate.

Again, however, Bentham's shadow falls over the enterprise. It seems highly unlikely that any such derivation could issue in anything very specific (as Rawls himself was drawn to accept), and yet, as we have seen, single-word freedoms and rights need specification. The edges need rubbing off: freedom of expression does not include slanderous speech or fraudulent speech, but what about harmful and offensive speech, and what if even harmless speech proves sufficiently unpopular for me to suffer professionally or socially? Single-word abstract rights are bound to come into conflict. In blasphemy, freedom of expression clashes with freedom of religion. How should it be decided when my right to a good night's sleep conflicts with the public's right to drive on the motorways twenty-four hours a day, or the airlines' right to choose journey times? And is not a good night's sleep after all more an aspiration than a right? Even the right to participate in the political process, often exhibited as the most fundamental, inalienable political right of all, might need qualifying. What if a large group will, if they participate in the political process, immediately dismantle it in favour of a theocracy in which almost nobody participates in any political process – might it not be legitimate to suspend the franchise? Nobody really thinks that highly abstract considerations about the rational self-consciousness or freedom of choice of individuals could settle such details. Rights are supposed to trump other practical considerations and lay down clear and definite rules. But once they have to submit themselves to weighing scales, assessed and balanced against an unknown number of competing rights, any clarity they promise disappears.

Imperialism, multiculturalism, community

This is perhaps just as well. If we were more confident of a kind of rational calculus of detailed rights, then the spectre of imperialism raises its head. For there will be communities and nations whose laws and customs do not conform to the detail we have managed to abstract for ourselves. One of Bentham's charges against the 'a prioristic' rationalist language of the French Declaration of Rights was that, if taken literally, it followed that no established government across the whole world was legitimate. In principle, therefore, it gave the revolutionaries a legal carte blanche to impose their own ideas about government on any of the other nations of Europe, or of the whole world, that they chose to target. Rights that are thought of as derivable from undeniable, general features of human life are then in danger of providing us, we who have had the wit to work them out, with a legitimate reason for interfering with those benighted others who have not. For we have reason on our side, and they do not. Seen in this light, the language of rights occupies something of the role of a new, proselytizing religion, impatient of the existence of infidels, anxious to globalize its own discoveries and to suppress whatever variations and alternatives have evolved elsewhere.

This is not, however, a retreat to 'communitarianism' or the kind of relativism that says that if a community has evolved some particular forms of government and law, then that must be right 'in their terms'. Communities old and new can be horrible to their marginalized, their oppressed, women, people of different religions, those of low caste, people stigmatized as 'the Other', beyond the pale, and refused the rights and privileges of those on the inside. We do not have to give our own budget of rights a 'metaphysical' backing to see genuine oppression and injustice for what they are. But what is wrong with bad societies is whatever makes them bad, and these are seldom errors of reason. The problem lies with people's hearts, their fears, envies, prejudices and historical enmities, rather than their heads.

The moral, as so often, is that we have to be careful. Ordinary talk of rights as established and enshrined in custom and law is fine. Advocating particular policies and changes is fine, and using the language of rights is a perfectly reasonable way of attempting to persuade each other of the merits of a policy. But thinking of rights, however cloudily, as affording some kind of metaphysical basis for our advocacy is not. And thinking of a calculus of rights, unique and visible to people of reason everywhere, is dangerous in many directions. Even if it is not, as Bentham thought, a recipe for anarchy, it is certainly a recipe for self-righteousness, and it substitutes a kind of arid scholasticism for any fully human and multi-dimensioned thought about the wisdom of laws and policies, and what is necessary to enable us to get along together. Let the buyer beware.

Is Death to be Feared?
The awful abyss of extinction

In the old Scottish ballad 'Macpherson's Lament' we learn how the cattle rustler and musician James Macpherson faced his execution:

> *So rantingly, so wantonly,*
> *So dauntingly went he,*
> *He played a tune and danced it round*
> *Beneath the gallows tree.*

We admire Macpherson, perhaps with amazement, because we all fear death, or at the very least, find it difficult not to do so. Yet the philosopher Epicurus had a pithy argument that death should not be feared:

> *Death is nothing to us, for that which is dissolved is without*
> *sensation; and that which lacks sensation is nothing to us.*

The big sleep

It is quite difficult to wrap our minds around the full meaning of the idea that death is nothing to us. Death is signified by a noun, and death comes for us, and finishes us off: according to the poet John Donne, death may be called proud, although he enjoins it not to be, and according to some religious thinkers, death can be conquered, although others doubt that. It can't be *nothing*, can it? But 'nothing' is itself a treacherous word, all too easily interpreted as denoting a particular kind of being: a Not-being. We saw Schopenhauer describing how finding that our lives are surrounded by nothing induces metaphysical anxiety, an existential dread that assails us whenever we try to contemplate the eternal abyss of Nothing (see *Why Is There Something and Not Nothing?*). Nothing can affect us badly, for instance when we are expecting something, and if we are so affected it may be difficult to believe that we are affected by nothing. We may want to put capital letters on it, to show that our fear is real enough: it sounds better to say that we are affected by Nothing. Some philosophers fear Nothing, whereas the others think there is nothing to be afraid of.

If we try to imagine death, we probably think of cold, of silence, of immobility: a state which then goes on, unchanging, for a very long time – for ever, in fact. The ultimate Big Sleep. And that may seem a rather grim prospect, even if the sleep in question is beautifully peaceful. But we have already put a foot wrong if we are on this path. We are trying to imagine what it will be like *for ourselves*, and that is a crucial false step. My death will be like nothing, for me, because there will be no 'me' left. It will not be like being cold, or silent, or immobile, or being in a hole in the ground, nor, if my body is cremated, will it be like being put in a fire. It will be like nothing. For me, that is. The world, of course, will go on being like it is, or perhaps changing, for everyone else who is still around.

Deceptive imaginings

When we imagine the scenes of life, we imagine ourselves having a perspective on them. Asked to imagine the Himalayas, I imagine what it would be like for me to see the Himalayas. If I imagine meeting the President or going scuba diving, I imagine the President looming into my field of view, or myself getting wet and blowing bubbles. The relentless presence of the first-person perspective infuses all our imaginings. But that is just what it must not do when we contemplate death. We have to erase ourselves altogether, and then imagination fails, because there is no first-person perspective on death. Nobody, ever, experiences it for themselves. If people are briefly dead, before they are resuscitated, then while they are dead they experience nothing (if they do, they're not dead, whatever they report when they come round).

Even if this is understood I suspect there is a lingering temptation to think that this necessary failure of imagination is not due to logic, but due to the mystery of the subject. If we cannot imagine what death is like, we think, then that must be because it is shrouded in mystery, and surely that makes it all the more fearful! This temptation should be resisted. 'Death' is no more mysterious than the 'state' of not yet being born. There will, next week and next year, be many people on earth who are not born yet, just as we ourselves were not born not so many years ago. Being unborn was not like anything, not because it was existing in some previous, but now hidden, way, but because there was no subject, no self, there at all. There were many thousands of millions of years before each of us existed, and there will doubtless be as many again after each of us has gone. We will be dead for a very long time, but it will not be boring, any more than it was boring waiting so long to be born. The final extinction of the solar system will happen exactly as quickly, as far as I am concerned, as the first summer after I die. I will have conquered time, but unfortunately I shall not enjoy my triumph, even for the blink of an eye.

Christians, concerned that the conventional image of heaven as endless hymn-singing is not actually all that appealing, sometimes try to say that the afterlife is timeless. In eternal life, they say, we shall have conquered time itself. But they then have to make sense of the difference between life outside time on the one hand, and extinction and oblivion on the other, and this cannot be done.

The false step we take when we try to imagine our own death is pregnant with consequences. Trying to do so, and finding it difficult, fuels fantasies of an afterlife. For look – here I am, imagining (say) my own funeral. There is no bodily me in the church, and the poor corpse in the coffin does not have this point of view. So it must be something ethereal, a ghostly shadow of myself, a soul in fact, hovering above the mourners, unhappily unable to tell them that I am fine after all, and awaiting new adventures in whatever kind of afterlife now beckons. It is strange how gripping this fantasy can be, while we do not think in the same way that since we can imagine witnessing the parental grapplings surrounding our conception, that we had a forelife as a soul, a spiritual or bleached-out version of what we now are.

Past and future

Philosophically, it is not entirely clear why there is this temporal asymmetry about our imaginings – the very word 'afterlife' appears in the dictionaries, but its logical twin, 'forelife', does not. People talk of kingdom come, but not of kingdom went. Perhaps the prejudice connects with other ways in which we live our lives forwards, but not backwards. We have to plot and plan and decide and take heed for the future, while the past is over and done. So the question, 'What *will* it be like *for me*?' is in general much nearer the forefront of our minds than the question, 'What *was* it like *for me*?' Perhaps we are hard-wired to take more heed for the future than for the past. And the way we do so is to play through scenarios in our mind's eye: scenes as they may be witnessed by ourselves, so that we can rehearse what to do, and prepare for eventualities.

This asymmetry between our experience of past and future affects how we think of our identity through time. Philosophers like to imagine fission and fusion cases, in which various kinds of splitting apart and coming together seem to affect who we are. Suppose, for instance, part of my brain were transplanted into another body, and another part into a different body, and that the resulting persons go off and live different lives. Imagining this future, there seems to be an urgent question: 'Where will *I* be?' If at a particular time one of these is in a silent red room and one in a noisy green room, then where will I be? It seems I must be one or the other, assuming I exist then. There is nobody at the later time for whom it is a bit like being in a silent red room and a bit like being in a noisy green room, so it seems there are three crisp alternatives: either I shall be in the one, or I shall be in the other, or I shall not have survived the transplants.

Yet if we play the same thought experiment backwards, our attachment to one crisp answer is not nearly so firm. Suppose I learn that my present brain is the result of a fusion of two or more different brains coming from different people. Fascinating. Suppose the possessor of one part was climbing Mont Blanc on midsummer day in the year 2000, while the other was munching chips on a sofa – where was I? If I can unambiguously remember doing one of those things, then I shall go with that one. If I can't, I might have a confused and scrambled memory, with fragments of a climb coming into my mind, but the taste of chips as well. I need not be too bothered: the question, 'Where was *I*?' is not nearly as urgent as in the parallel question for the future.

It might be some consolation, if we ever face the real prospect of a fission operation, to reflect that neither of the emerging people need be particularly bothered about whether they were once me. If one of them says that it was he who wrote these words, and the other says that no, it was he who did so, their quarrel is a topic of amusement, or a legal wrangle about royalties, rather than an intellectual problem that has to be solved, or that admits solution. It is a case where if need arises we can just legislate.

It is notable as well that the crispness of the question, 'Where will I be?' only belongs to the issue considered from the first-person point of view. If *you* become fragmented in the same way, then we can quite well cope with the thought that each of the resulting persons is a bit like you. Perhaps one has your engaging sense of humour, while the other has your quick capacity for logic. Perhaps one is better at remembering the football games we saw together, while the other accompanies my singing, just as you did. It might be emotionally a bit disorienting, but there is no insistent question about which is you, any more than if I dismantle my bicycle and cleverly reassemble the parts into two distinct bicycles there is an insistent question about which is the original. The question of identity might trouble the law, for example if the tax on new bicycles is different from the tax on old ones, but it need not trouble the metaphysician. Similarly, the question of which of two resulting persons is, say, my wife who went in for the operation, might have legal rather than philosophical interest, especially as bigamy is illegal.

Taking it lightly?

Returning to death, is the fact that it is nothing to us an invitation to take it lightly? In many respects it retains its awful gravity. The end of a life is a significant event, after all. Causing it may be one of the most serious of crimes, and evading it is one of our principal concerns. If you push me off a cliff you deserve the penalties of the law, and if I am about to walk off a cliff, and you save me at the last moment, you deserve my gratitude. Is all this importance difficult to reconcile with Epicurus's lesson?

Surely not. Looking ahead to my own extinction, I may very much hope to avoid it, but not because I am comparing what it will be like for me if I manage to avoid it, with what it will be like for me if I do not. There is no second point of comparison. But I may very much hope to avoid it simply because of what it will be like for me if I do so. Very likely, I gain something I very much want. I want to see the spring and hear the birds or be with my children or finish a book. If I die, I shall do none of those things, and that might reasonably bother me a great deal. A life cut off when full of anticipation and purpose is a real matter of sorrow, but what we mourn is the extinction of the subject's plans and joys, rather than the 'state' to which he or she has been reduced. The death of someone young is much more of a tragedy than the death of someone elderly, just because the child's life was brimful of the prospects that will never materialize, whereas the elderly life is not. We feel the loss much more, and rightly so. But it is we who mourn it, not the dead, who mourn nothing.

Because we are social animals and in normal conditions concerned with the preservation of friends and family, or even acquaintances and strangers, murder inspires us with horror and fear, and it is good that it does so. After all, our own self-preservation is a leading concern for each of us. A different concern we have is for our own dignity and our own capacity to control our lives, and to keep ourselves free from pain and distress. But nature is cruel, and these two concerns can clash. When the subject's life is intolerable and is expected to remain so, the desire for self-preservation may give way, and suicide may be the desired way out. It is unfortunate, of course, but the misfortune lies in whatever torments make it the preferred option. Yet it has been a constant target of condemnation from religious bodies. Somewhat illogically, the same priests who promise a blissful afterlife forbid this mode of achieving it as sacrilegious, as 'playing God', as betraying the sanctity of life, and declaim that while they themselves are unfortunately unable to punish anyone successfully performing such an act,

God most certainly will. Meanwhile, although baffled of a defendant to charge, they have had to content themselves with inflicting their indignities on the successful suicide in his absence, for instance by defaming his memory as shameful, by denying his corpse the rites of burial, or by persecuting anyone merciful enough to have assisted him.

As usual, the most elegant dismissal of this superstition comes from David Hume, in his famous 1755 essay 'Of Suicide'. Hume points out that nature operates on fixed and unalterable general laws and that human animals, like others, have a basket of capacities with which to cope with the circumstances in which we find ourselves. If those capacities suggest self-annihilation, this is no more contrary to the ways of the cosmos, and hence the ways of any Supreme Being who brings it about or sustains it, than any other exercise of our powers:

> 'Tis impious, says the French superstition, to inoculate for the small-pox, or usurp the business of providence by voluntarily producing distempers and maladies. 'Tis impious, says the modern European superstition, to put a period to our own life, and thereby rebel against our Creator; and why not impious, say I, to build houses, cultivate the ground, or sail upon the ocean? In all these actions we employ our powers of mind and body, to produce some innovation in the course of nature; and in none of them do we any more.

If we 'play God' when we take our own life, then we equally play God when we dig a garden or put up an umbrella. Hume then turns his attention to the fatuous idea that nature has, as it were,

placed me at my post like a sentinel, so that it is an abandon-
ment of my duty if I desert it:

> 'Tis providence surely that has placed me at this present in
> this chamber: But may I not leave it when I think proper,
> without being liable to the imputation of having deserted my
> post or station? When I shall be dead, the principles of which
> I am composed will still perform their part in the universe,
> and will be equally useful in the grand fabrick, as when they
> composed this individual creature. The difference to the whole
> will be no greater than between my being in a chamber and
> in the open air. The one change is of more importance to me
> than the other; but not more so to the universe.

Nature has given us a horror of death, sure enough. But nature
has also given many people a horror of spiders or snakes, which
they manage to overcome.

It may indeed be one's duty to try to dissuade a would-be suicide: perhaps life is not so intolerable; perhaps it is going to
improve, and perhaps he or she will live to be thankful that they
resisted the temptation, and put up with their current misfortune for a while longer. But if these persuasions fail – and after
all, in fearsome cases of terminal illness and incurable pain they
may be very hollow – and the victim decides to fall upon his own
sword, then it is impossible to see that any wrong has been done.
I suppose that most of us hope that, like Macpherson, we will
face death bravely, and it is surely admirable to fear indignity,
pain, distress and becoming a heavy burden on loved ones more
than death itself, in which case it is also admirable to plan that if

and when these horrors descend upon us, we will be able to exit more gracefully than nature, left to its own devices, will enable us to do.

Since we owe each other duties of care, and killing ourselves is very difficult, it may even be the duty of sympathetic carers to help. The alternative is often an agonizing process of dying, when careful help would make everything much easier for all. Yet, extraordinarily, the law in the United Kingdom and in most states in the USA places such assistance on very much the same footing as murder. The only reason ever given, apart from the kinds of superstition that Hume destroys, is that people might feel 'pressured' to ask for death by others who are selfishly eager to see them go. Clearly there have to be safeguards, but equally clearly in jurisdictions where it is permissible to assist suicide, such safeguards work perfectly well.

Not-being

I have talked throughout of death as extinction, and ignored the alleged possibility of an afterlife. I believe that we are only tempted to think we can make sense of this idea because of the mistake about imagination that we have already confronted. Mankind's long obsession with existence in the hereafter is the result of a philosophical error. Some may think that they can satisfactorily model an afterlife on this one: the soul is then a kind of ghost, a shadowy version of a person, the kind of things that people claim to see, and which appear to them to be ambassadors from the world of the dead (although it is quite significant that since ghosts tend to be fully dressed, their clothes are presumably also shadowy ambassadors from the realm of dead sheets and dead suits of armour).

As projections of our own mental states, these phenomena may be real enough: a house in which a partner or child has died is indeed haunted by their absence, that is, by the aching awareness in those living that the partner or child is no longer there, and consequently by the disturbing imagining that they still are. But being haunted by an absence is not being haunted by a kind of thing, any more than the absence of crocodiles in England is itself a kind of thing, an ambassador from the shadowy world of Not-being of English crocodiles.

It is nothing so mysterious, only the quite unmysterious fact that there is nothing, whether person or crocodile. In cases where until recently there was something or someone, that may itself be something terrible to lament and mourn. I suppose I secretly hope, like many others, that friends and family will be at least a little sad when it happens to me, which I hope will happen only after a benign old age pottering around and correcting my philosophical works. But for myself, it will be nothing about which I will be bothered.

Notes

1. Am I a Ghost in a Machine?

For Descartes on the pilot analogy, see his *Meditation* 6 (Descartes's *Meditations* are available in many editions). Ryle's phrase is from *The Concept of Mind* (Chicago: University of Chicago Press, 1949), pp. 15–16.

For Locke, see his *Essay Concerning Human Understanding*, ed. P.H. Nidditch (Oxford: Oxford University Press, 1975), bk II, ch. viii, sect. 13, p. 136. For Leibniz, see *New Essays on Human Understanding*, tr. and ed. Peter Remnant and Jonathan Bennett (Cambridge: Cambridge University Press, 1996), bk II, ch. viii, 131. Leibniz's essay is a detailed response to Locke's.

Jackson first unveiled Mary in 'Epiphenomenal Qualia', *Philosophical Quarterly* 32: (1982) pp. 127–36. However, he repudiates the argument in chapter 12 of *The Oxford Handbook of Contemporary Philosophy* (Oxford: Oxford University Press, 2007), which he edited together with Michael Smith.

The brilliant argument from Wittgenstein occurs in *Philosophical Investigations* (Oxford: Blackwell, 1953), §§243–320. The exact interpretation of all his remarks is a minor philosophical industry in itself. There is a good discussion in Robert Fogelin, *Wittgenstein* (London: Routledge, 1976), ch. 13. A more complex recent treatment is in Stephen Mulhall, *Wittgenstein's Private Language: Grammar, Nonsense and Imagination in Philosophical Investigations*, (Oxford: Oxford University Press, 2007) §§ 243–315.

The phrase 'the explanatory gap' is due to Joe Levine, whose book *Purple Haze: The Puzzle of Consciousness* (Oxford: Oxford University Press, 2001) can be recommended. Excellent introductions to the philosophy of mind include Tim Crane, *Elements of Mind* (Oxford: Oxford University Press, 2001). A good guide to several theories is William Seager, *Theories of Consciousness* (London: Routledge, 1999). For Aristotle on mind and body, see his *De Anima*.

2. What Is Human Nature?

See Dawkins, *The Selfish Gene* (Oxford: Oxford University Press, 1976), ch. 11. For work prioritizing genetic endowment over environment, see Stephen Pinker, *The Blank Slate: The Modern Denial of Human Nature* (London: Allen Lane, 2002). For hair-raising pronouncements on human nature in the light of biology, see M.T. Ghiselin, *The Economy of Nature and the Evolution of Sex* (Berkeley: University of California Press, 1974). A more nuanced account is in E. Jablonka and M. Lamb, *Evolution in Four Dimensions* (Cambridge, Mass.: MIT Press, 2005).

The classic refutation of psychological egoism is given in Bishop Joseph Butler, *Fifteen Sermons Preached at the Rolls Chapel*, ed. Revd. D. Matthews (London: Bell & Son, 1974), especially sermons 5 and 6. I discuss Butler in *Ruling Passions* (Oxford: Oxford University Press, 1998), pp. 137–60.

For a more extended meditation on the difference between sexual desire and the desire to procreate, see my *Lust* (New York: Oxford University Press, 2004).

In classical philosophy, accounts of the unity of the virtues appear in Plato's dialogues, especially *Republic*, *Protagoras* and *Laches*, and in Aristotle's *Nicomachaean Ethics*, bk VI.

3. Am I Free?

'The Dilemma of Determinism' was the title of a celebrated lecture by William James, easily available on the web. An early, and classic, refutation of the idea that we are conscious of free will is in Schopenhauer's essay *On the Freedom of the Will* (Oxford: Blackwell, 1985), p. 43.

Michael Frayn's lament occurs in *The Human Touch: Our Part in the Creation of a Universe* (London: Faber and Faber, 2006), p. 394.

Benjamin Libet summarizes his work in *Mind Time: The Temporal Factor in Consciousness* (Cambridge, Mass.: Harvard University Press, 2004).

The classic paper on the place of reactive emotions in human life, and the way they mediate our interactions with each other, is Peter Strawson, 'Freedom and Resentment', in his collection *Freedom and Resentment and Other Essays* (London: Methuen, 1974).

4. What Do We Know?

Plato's account of knowledge as justified true belief occurs in the dialogue *Theaetetus*.

Edmund Gettier published his minuscule article 'Is Justified True Belief Knowledge?' in *Analysis* 26 (1963). For subsequent reactions, consult E. Sosa and J. Kim, eds., *Epistemology: An Anthology* (Oxford: Blackwell, 2000).

There is not much philosophical work that addresses the question of the purpose in having a concept of knowledge in the first place. The shining exception is E. Craig, *Knowledge and the State of Nature: An Essay in Conceptual Synthesis* (Oxford: Oxford University Press, 1999).

The relation between experience, scepticism and thought can be pursued in Michael Williams, *Problems of Knowledge* (Oxford: Oxford University Press, 2001).

Popper's views were first revealed in 1934 in his wildly successful book *The Logic of Scientific Discovery* (London: Routledge Classics, 2002).

5. Are We Rational Animals?

Hume's scepticism about the powers of reason pretty much pervades his *Treatise of Human Nature*, originally published in 1739–40. For reasons about reasoning, see bk I, pt iv, sect. 1. For reason and passion, see bk II, pt iii, sect. 3.

The distinction between a priori and a posteriori is pivotal in Kant's 1781 masterpiece, *The Critique of Pure Reason*. Conventionalism about the geometrical description of the world is found in J.H. Poincaré, *Science and Hypothesis* (London: Dover Books, 1952). The theory applied to logical necessity is found in logical positivist writing, such as Rudolf Carnap's *Logical Syntax of Language* (New

York: Open Court Classics, 2002), or A.J. Ayer, *Language, Truth and Logic* (London: Gollancz, 1936), ch. 4. Ludwig Wittgenstein flirts with conventionalism in *Remarks on the Foundations of Mathematics* (Oxford: Blackwell, 1956). Attacks on conventionalism include W.V. Quine, 'Carnap and Logical Truth', in his *The Ways of Paradox and Other Essays* (Cambridge, Mass.: Harvard University Press, 1976). The view that a priori truths are merely those to which we are most attached is suggested in Quine's classic essay 'Two Dogmas of Empiricism', in his *From a Logical Point of View* (Cambridge, Mass.: Harvard University Press, 1952).

Practical reasons make up the whole field of moral philosophy. In recent years influential treatments emphasizing reason have included C. Korsgaard, *Sources of Normativity* (Cambridge: Cambridge University Press, 1996), and T.M. Scanlon, *What We Owe to Each Other* (Cambridge, Mass.: Harvard University Press, 2000).

6. How Can I Lie to Myself?

The Sartre quotation is from *Being and Nothingness: An Essay on Phenomenological Ontology*, tr. Hazel E. Barnes (London: Routledge, 1969), p. 49. Pascal's wager is from his *Pensées*, tr. A. J. Krailsheimer (London: Penguin, 1966), pp. 149–55.

Mark Johnston's paper 'Self-Deception and the Nature of Mind' is included in the best single collection on the topic, *Perspectives on Self-Deception*, ed. Brian McLaughlin and Amélie Rorty (Berkeley: University of California Press, 1988). The quotation in the text is from p. 64. Other valuable papers in this collection include those by the editors and by Bas van Fraassen, Allen Wood and Georges Rey. There are also perceptive comments on literary studies of self-deception. Davidson's view is in his 'Paradoxes of Irrationality', in R. Wollheim and J. Hopkins, eds., *Philosophical Essays on Freud* (Cambridge: Cambridge University Press, 1982), pp. 289–305.

Other good books include Al Mele, *Self-Deception Unmasked* (Princeton: Princeton University Press, 2001), and D. Pears, *Motivated Irrationality* (New York: Oxford University Press, 1984).

7. Is There Such a Thing as Society?

Mrs Thatcher's remark and its consequences are discussed in Nick Davies, *Dark Heart: The Shocking Truth about Hidden Britain* (London: Chatto & Windus, 1997).

The Locke quotation is from *Two Treatises of Civil Government*, ch. 7,)p. 93. The Hobbes quotation is from *Leviathan*, ch. 14.

For coyote behaviour, see C. Allen, and M. Bekoff, 'Animal Play and the Evolution of Morality: An Ethological Approach', *Topoi* 24 (2005), pp. 125–35.

The Darwin quotation is from *The Descent of Man and Selection in Relation to Sex*, p. 166. The best-known defence of the propriety of thinking biologically in terms of groups is *Unto Others*, by Elliott Sober and Alan Sloan Wilson (Cambridge, Mass.: Harvard University Press, 1998).

Robert Axelrod's experiment is described in his *The Evolution of Cooperation* (New York: Basic Books, 1984). Although Axelrod's result has become pivotal, its importance has been questioned by others immersed in the complexities of game theory. See Brian Skyrms, *The Stag Hunt and the Evolution of Social Structure* (Cambridge: Cambridge University Press, 2004), and K. Binmore, *Playing Fair: Game Theory and the Social Contract*, vol. 1 (Cambridge, Mass.: MIT Press, 1994).

For experimental economics, see V.L. Smith, *Rationality in Economics: Constructive and Ecological Forms* (New York: Cambridge University Press, 2008); C. Bicchieri, *The Grammar of Society* (Cambridge: Cambridge University Press, 2006).

The Keynes quotation is from *The General Theory of Employment, Interest and Money* (1934), ch. 24.

8. Can We Understand Each Other?

Locke's discussion occurs in his *Essay Concerning Human Understanding*, ed. P.H. Nidditch (Oxford: Oxford University Press, 1975), bk III, ch. 2. Locke is defended in Michael Ayers, *Locke* (London: Routledge, 1991).

Wittgenstein's knock-down argument comes in *The Blue and Brown Books* (Oxford: Blackwell, 1964), p. 3.

Madeleine Bassett's views are seen to advantage in *Right Ho, Jeeves*, by P.G. Wodehouse. Bertie Wooster queries their consistency in ch. 10.

Aristotle tells of Cratylus in *Metaphysics* Γ, 1010a7–15.

Humpty Dumpty expounds his view of language in *Alice Through the Looking Glass*, ch. 6.

Davidson's argument is in 'On the Very Idea of a Conceptual Scheme', in his *Inquiries into Truth and Interpretation* (Oxford:

Oxford University Press, 1984). Davidson's work has prompted volumes of discussion, including J.E. Malpas, *Donald Davidson and the Mirror of Meaning* (Cambridge: Cambridge University Press, 1992), and Bjorn Ramberg, *Donald Davidson's Philosophy of Language: An Introduction* (Oxford: Blackwell, 1989).

9. Can Machines Think?

Turing's classic paper 'Computing Machinery and Intelligence' appeared in the journal *Mind* in 1950 and has been much anthologized.

There are excellent introductions to the topic of this chapter, including Tim Crane, *The Mechanical Mind* (London: Routledge, 2003); Jack Copeland, *Artificial Intelligence: A Philosophical Introduction* (Oxford: Blackwell, 1993); John Searle, *Intentionality* (Cambridge: Cambridge University Press, 1983); John Haugeland, *Artificial Intelligence: The Very Idea* (Cambridge, Mass.: MIT Press, 1985). A good collection of important early discussions is Margaret Boden, ed., *The Philosophy of Artificial Intelligence* (Oxford: Oxford University Press, 1990).

Dreyfus's criticism of the programme of AI is in *What Computers Still Can't Do* (Cambridge, Mass.: MIT Press, 1992).

John Searle propounded the Chinese room thought experiment in 'Minds, Brains and Programs', in the journal *Behavioral and Brain Sciences* 3 (1980), pp. 417–24.

Dennett's collection *Brainstorms* (Hassocks: Harvester Press, 1979) and his *The Intentional Stance* (Cambridge, Mass.: Bradford Books, 1989) are fertile sources of arguments and examples.

10. Why Be Good?

The myth of the ring of Gyges comes in book II of Plato's *Republic*, 360b. I discuss it at greater length in my *Plato's Republic* (London: Atlantic Books, 2006).

The quotation from David Hume is in *An Enquiry Concerning the Principles of Morals*, ed. Tom L. Beauchamp (Oxford: Oxford University Press, 1998), p. 125.

For egoism, see the work by Joseph Butler cited in the notes to chapter 2.

The famous example of an apparent sense of injustice in animals is reported in S.J. Brosnan and F.B.M. de Waal, 'Monkeys Reject Unequal Pay', *Nature* 425 (2003), pp. 297–99.

The quotation from Machiavelli is in *The Prince*, tr. George Bull (Harmondsworth: Penguin Classics, 1961), p. 100.

The Newcastle result is reported in M. Bateson, D. Nettle and G. Roberts, 'Cues of Being Watched Enhance Cooperation in a Real-World Setting', *Biology Letters* 2.3 (2006), pp. 412–14.

11. Is It All Relative?

Many of the themes of this chapter are treated at greater length in my *Truth: A Guide for the Perplexed* (London: Allen Lane, 2005), which also gives fuller references to the literature.

The classic defence of deflationism is Paul Horwich, *Truth*, 2nd ed. (Oxford: Oxford University Press, 1998).

12. Does Time Go By?

The quote from St Augustine comes in *The Confessions*, tr. Philip Burton (London: Everyman, 2001), ch. 11.14.17, p. 271.

Huw Price's discussion is in his *Time's Arrow and Archimedes' Point* (New York: Oxford University Press, 1996). The long quotation is from p. 14. Other forceful defences of the block universe standpoint include Hugh Mellor, *Real Time II* (London: Routledge, 1998). An excellent general introduction is Michael Lockwood, *The Labyrinth of Time* (Oxford: Oxford University Press, 2005).

Kant talks of the forms of inner and outer sense in *The Critique of Pure Reason*, B67–70. For backwards causation, see Price, pp. 242–48.

Time travel is the theme of many sci-fi books and films. A classic, with paradoxes well in view, is Robert A. Heinlein, 'By His Bootstraps', in his collection *The Menace from the Earth* (New York: Gnome Press, 1959).

13. Why Do Things Keep On Keeping On?

Popper's views are stated in *Conjectures and Refutations* (London: Routledge Classics, 2002).

Martin Rees's book is *Just Six Numbers: The Deep Forces that Shape our Universe* (London: Weidenfeld & Nicolson, 1999).

Hume's remarks about natural science come in *An Enquiry Concerning Human Understanding*, ed. Tom L. Beauchamp (Oxford: Oxford University Press, 1999), pp. 111–12.

The idea of a sustaining deity is perhaps slightly less familiar than the idea of a creating deity. The first cause argument is more familiar than an argument to a kind of Atlas that continuously supports the order of the whole cosmos. But they are close cousins, and each is equally a version of what is known as the cosmological argument. Indeed, in some philosophers, most notably Descartes, the doctrine of 'continuous creation' identifies them (Descartes, *Discourse on Method*, IV; *Meditations*, III). On this account the deity creates the universe anew each moment, fortunately keeping track of what it was like the previous moment and then making the slightly different world; a process that we interpret as smooth changes in the one world.

Wittgenstein's aphorism is from a slightly different context, in *Philosophical Investigations* §304, p. 102.

14. Why Is There Something and Not Nothing?

The quote from Leibniz is in *Principles of Nature and Grace Founded on Reason*, in G.W. Leibniz, *Philosophical Essays*, ed. Roger Ariew and Daniel Garber (Indianapolis: Hackett, 1989), p. 209.

Schopenhauer's passage occurs in *The World as Will and Representation*, tr. E.F.J. Payne (New York: Dover Books, 1958), vol. 2, ch. 17, p. 161.

Hume's discussion of Leibniz's argument comes in his *Dialogues Concerning Natural Religion*, pt IX. There are many editions of this marvellous work.

St Augustine's discussion is in *The Confessions*, tr. Philip Burton (London: Everyman, 2001), bk 11. The flippant reply is cited in 11.12.14, p. 269.

If we take ignorance to licence distributions of probabilities the numbers quickly get out of hand. Physicist Roger Penrose is reported to have calculated a probability of an initial state organized to produce things like us as one in 10 to the power of 10 to the power of 123: a big number by any standards.

For Kant on the regulative versus constitutive distinction, see *The Critique of Pure Reason*, A508, B536: 'The Regulative Principle of Pure Reason in Its Application to the Cosmological Ideas.'

15. What Fills Up Space?

I broached this question in 'Filling in Space' in *Analysis* (1990), pp. 62–65.

Kant's worry comes in *The Critique of Pure Reason*, A284, B340. The best commentary on Kant's use of these ideas is Rae Langton, *Kantian Humility: Our Ignorance of Things in Themselves* (Oxford: Oxford University Press, 2001).

Michael Faraday's discussion is in 'A Speculation Touching Electrical Conduction and the Nature of Matter', in *Experimental Researches in Electricity*, vol. 2 (London: Richard and John Edward Taylor, 1844). I owe the quotation to Langton, p. 181.

Bertrand Russell's not-just-washing argument is in his *The Analysis of Matter* (London: Kegan Paul, 1927), p. 325.

The usefulness of possible worlds for thinking about conditionals was influentially revealed in David Lewis, *Counterfactuals* (Oxford: Blackwell, 1973).

For dispositions and their 'grounds' in categoricals, see Stephen Mumford, *Dispositions* (Oxford: Oxford University Press, 1998).

The quotation from Newton is in a letter to Richard Bentley, cited in Norman Kemp Smith, *The Philosophy of David Hume* (London: Macmillan, 1942), p. 61.

16. What Is Beauty?

Works that might be consulted on beauty include Mary Mothersill, *Beauty Restored* (Oxford: Oxford University Press, 1984); Roger Scruton, *Beauty* (Oxford: Oxford University Press, 2009); W. Steiner, *Venus in Exile: The Flight from Beauty in Twentieth-Century Art* (Chicago: Chicago University Press, 2002); Malcolm Budd, *Values of Art: Pictures, Poetry and Music* (Harmondsworth: Penguin, 1997).

Kant explores the antinomy of taste in *The Critique of Judgment*, tr. James Meredith (Oxford: Oxford University Press, 1952), bk II, pt 1, §36, p. 144.

The Wordsworth quotation is from 'Ode: Intimations of Immortality from Recollections of Early Childhood'.

Kant, 'there can be no rule', is from *The Critique of Judgment*, bk I, pt 1, §9, p. 56.

Hume's discussion is in his essay 'Of the Standard of Taste', in *Essays, Moral, Political, and Literary*, ed. Eugene F. Miller (Indianapolis: Liberty Fund, 1985), vol. 1, essay 23. Rousseau's view comes in his book *Émile, or Education*. The Woodhouse story occurs in the collection *Very Good, Jeeves*.

Kant, 'By an aesthetic idea', is from *The Critique of Judgment*, bk II, pt 1, §49, p. 177.

The Shakespeare quotation is from *The Merchant of Venice*, V.i.83–8. The Schiller quotation is from *Letters on the Aesthetic Education of Man*, Letter 2.

17. Do We Need God?

Hume's *Dialogues Concerning Natural Religion* were published in 1779, only after his death, and are available in many editions.

Schopenhauer's passage occurs in *The World as Will and Representation*, tr. E.F.J. Payne (New York: Dover, 1958), vol. 2, ch. 17, p. 166.

Amartya Sen recounts his grandfather's reaction in *The Argumentative Indian* (London: Allen Lane, 2005), p. 46.

I owe the figures about differential cohesion of religious and non-religious groups to a lecture by evolutionary anthropologist William Irons, at the London School of Economics in 2007.

A good survey of some of the psychological findings occurs in Azim Sharif and Ara Norenzayan, 'God is Watching You', *Psychological Studies* 18, no. 9 (2007).

18. What Is It All For?

My discussion in this chapter echoes material in my essay 'Religion and Respect', in Louise Antony, ed., *Philosophers Without Gods* (New York: Oxford University Press, 2007).

The quote from Voltaire is in *Candide*, ch. 30 (the last page of the book).

F.P. Ramsey talks about his size in his *Philosophical Papers*, ed. D.H. Mellor (Cambridge: Cambridge University Press, 1990), p. 249.

For an attempt to portray the change from a religious to a secular world view as merely substituting a religion of progress for a proper religion, see John Gray, *Gray's Anatomy* (London: Allen Lane, 2009).

For our problems as custodians of our own interests or our own happiness, see Daniel M. Haybron, *The Pursuit of Unhappiness* (Oxford: Oxford University Press, 2008).

19. What Are My Rights?

The quotations from Bentham in this chapter are from his *Anarchical Fallacies: Being an Examination of the Declaration of Rights Issued During the French Revolution*. This short text is most easily available on the web. For other critics of natural rights, including Marx, see Jeremy Waldron, *Nonsense on Stilts: Bentham, Burke and Marx on the Rights of Man* (London: Routledge, 1988).

For the extension of rights to animals, see Tom Regan, *The Case for Animal Rights* (Berkeley: University of California Press, 1983). For 'deep' ecology and surrounding issues, see Patrick Curry, *Ecological Ethics: An Introduction* (Cambridge: Polity Press, 2005).

Multiculturalism, the politics of identity and liberalism are well discussed by Anthony Appiah in *The Ethics of Identity* (Princeton: Princeton University Press, 2007), and in *Cosmopolitanism: Ethics in a World of Strangers* (London: Penguin, 2007).

20. Is Death to be Feared?

The pithy argument from Epicurus is in *Principal Doctrines*, II, in *Epicurus: The Extant Remains*, tr. Cyril Bailey (Oxford: Oxford University Press, 1926), p. 95.

Thought experiments about personal identity make up much of part 3 of Derek Parfit's *Reasons and Persons* (Oxford: Oxford University Press, 1984), leading Parfit to conclusions echoing those of David Hume in his *Treatise*, bk I, pt IV, sect. 6. Other well-known discussions of death include Jay Rosenberg, *Thinking Clearly About Death* (Indianapolis: Hackett, 1998), and Thomas Nagel, *Mortal Questions* (New York: Cambridge University Press, 1979).

David Hume, 'Of Suicide', is available in many collections, and published separately by Penguin Books in their Great Ideas series (2005).

The positive Dutch experience of transparency, public oversight and legal control was reported in Onwuteaka-Philipsen et al., *British Medical Journal* 331 (2005), pp. 691–93.

Key Philosophers

Aristotle (384–322 BC) Greek philosopher; along with *Plato the most influential philosopher of the western tradition.

Augustine of Hippo, St (354–430) Major Christian philosopher and theologian, and a key figure in the transition from pagan to specifically Christian philosophy.

Bentham, Jeremy (1748–1832) English philosopher of law, language and ethics, and notable early utilitarian.

Berkeley, George (1685–1753) Irish idealist and critic of Locke.

Butler, Joseph (1692–1752) English moral philosopher, and Bishop of Durham.

Cratylus (5th century BC) Greek philosopher, sometimes thought to have been a teacher of Plato before Socrates.

Davidson, Donald Herbert (1917–2003) American philosopher, notable for influential essays in the philosophy of mind and language.

Dennett, Daniel Clement (1942–) American philosopher of mind and of evolution.

Descartes, René (1596–1650) French mathematician and founding father of modern philosophy.

Dreyfus, Hubert (1929–) American philosopher specializing in phenomenology and existentialism, and critic of artificial intelligence.

Epicurus (341–270 BC) Greek philosopher, notable for a materialist view of nature, and independence from religion.

Gettier, Edmund (1927–) American philosopher known for his work on the problem of defining knowledge.

Heraclitus of Ephesus (d. after 480 BC) Shadowy Greek philosopher, known for his doctrine of the 'flux' or ceaseless change of all things.

Hobbes, Thomas (1588–1679) English philosopher, mathematician and linguist, best remembered for his analysis of the origins of civil society from the state of nature.

Hume, David (1711–76) Hugely influential Scottish philosopher, historian and essayist. Hume is the most important thoroughgoing naturalist in modern philosophy.

Jackson, Frank (1943–) Wide-ranging Australian philosopher of mind and metaphysics.

James, William (1842–1910) American psychologist and philosopher noted for his pragmatism and works on psychology; brother of novelist Henry James.

Johnston, Mark Contemporary Australian philosopher based in Princeton. His work covers ethics, philosophy of mind, metaphysics and philosophical logic.

Kant, Immanuel (1724–1804) Hugely influential German philosopher, whose masterpiece *The Critique of Pure Reason* set the agenda for much subsequent work.

Leibniz, Gottfried Wilhelm (1646–1716) German rationalist metaphysician, mathematician and polymath.

Locke, John (1632–1704) Influential early empiricist whose *Essay*

Concerning Human Understanding profoundly influenced subsequent 18th-century thought.

Machiavelli, Niccolò (1469–1527) Florentine political philosopher, notorious for his unflinching realism in analysing the nature of power in politics.

Marx, Karl (1818–83) German founder of revolutionary communism, and the most influential analyst and critic of capitalism and its effects on labour.

Pascal, Blaise (1623–62) French mathematician, physicist, and philosopher.

Plato (*c.* 429–347 BC) Together with Aristotle the most influential philosopher of the western tradition, whose *Dialogues* explore almost all subsequent branches of philosophical thought.

Popper, Karl Raimund (1902–94) Viennese-born philosopher of science, notable for his emphasis on falsifiability at the expense of confirmation and probability in science.

Price, Huw Contemporary Australian philosopher and influential pragmatist and philosopher of physics and time.

Rawls, John (1921–2002) American moral and political philosopher, whose work *A Theory of Justice* rekindled political philosophy and set the agenda for the last third of the 20th century.

Rousseau, Jean-Jacques (1712–78) French philosopher, influential before the Revolution and early critic of the Enlightenment.

Russell, Bertrand Arthur William (1872–1970) English empiricist philosopher, first notable for work in logic and the philosophy of language, and later for social and political ideas.

Ryle, Gilbert (1900–76) English philosopher and classicist.

Sartre, Jean Paul (1905–80) French existentialist philosopher and novelist, and the dominant French intellectual of his time.

Schiller, Johann Cristoph Friedrich (1759–1805) German poet and
man of letters, remembered philosophically principally for his
influential insistence on the importance of aesthetics.

Schopenhauer, Arthur (1788–1860) German philosopher and
Anglophile critic of Kant and Hegel. His work is often seen as
having affinities with Buddhism, recommending resignation and
extinction.

Searle, John (1932–) American philosopher of language and
of mind.

Smith, Adam (1723–90) Scottish polymath. Although best remembered as an economist, Smith was an eminent social theorist and
moral philosopher.

Socrates (469–399 BC) The relentless questioning figure of the early
dialogues of Plato, famous eventually for his virtue
and stoicism.

Strawson, Peter Frederick (1919–2006) English philosopher influential in bringing metaphysical interests back into the
Anglo-American philosophical world.

Voltaire (1694–1778) French man of letters and philosopher, and
leading figure of the Enlightenment in France.

Wittgenstein, Ludwig (1889–1951) Viennese-born philosopher
who worked mainly in Cambridge, and dominated English
philosophy for much of the 20th century.

Index